Callie's Tally

Betsy Howie

~

Jeremy P. Tarcher/Penguin

a member of Penguin Group (USA) Inc. New York

Callie's Tally

~

An Accounting of Baby's First Year

(Or: What My Daughter Owes Me)

Most Tarcher/Penguin books are available at special quantity discounts for bulk purchases for sales promotions, premiums, fund-raising, and educational needs. Special books or book excerpts also can be created to fit specific needs. For details, write Penguin Group (USA) Inc. Special Markets, 375 Hudson Street, New York, NY 10014.

Jeremy P. Tarcher/Penguin
a member of
Penguin Group (USA) Inc.
375 Hudson Street
New York, NY 10014
www.penguin.com

Library of Congress Cataloging-in-Publication Data

Howie, Betsy.
Callie's tally : an accounting of baby's first year, (or: what my daughter owes me) / by Betsy Howie.
p.   cm.
ISBN 1-58542-175-8
1. Howie, Betsy.   2. Mothers—Biography.
3. Childbirth—Costs.   4. Infants—Care—Costs.
5. Mother and infant—Humor.   I. Title.
HQ759.H782   2002   2002022688
306.874'3'092—dc21
ISBN 1-58542-247-9 (paperback ISBN)

Printed in the United States of America
1   3   5   7   9   10   8   6   4   2

BOOK DESIGN BY AMANDA DEWEY

for Callie

i.o.u.

ACKNOWLEDGMENTS

TO: ALL CREDITORS (including but not limited to): Mary Lou Howie, Lonnie, Chuck Howie, Wendy Stock, Sarah Howie, Randy Howie, Tim Howie, Evelyn Carter, Nic, Felicia, Eve, Wendy Hubbert, Elaine Markson, Gary Johnson, Kay Bishop, Joshua Jaffe, Howie Mortman, Robert Schnurr, Malcolm Brown, Scott Cady, Suzanne Presto, Julie Joseph, Liz Loftus, Judy Newman, David Vozar, Linda Dickey, Maggie Kneip, Ann Martin, Laura Godwin, Paula Danziger, Judy Marks, Kathleen Skutch, Julia Devlin, Fred Balling, Erica Joncyk, Cookie Kubarek, Jesse Walker and family, Bob Kirsch, Tory Jadow, Martha Miller, Gloria Parker, Christine Berglund, Xanny Garcia, Eric Weaver, Paula Wood, the staff at Mountainside and FV.

FROM: BETSY HOWIE

RE: UNPAYABLE DEBT

I am buried in debt.

And it's not the kind I can pay off by stashing away

the odd nickel to make slow but regular payments until everyone agrees that the balance is 0. No, this debt is not directly reimbursable. These are the kinds of chits that can only be buried by kind deeds, clean living, and good acts of humble gratitude.

My only hope of paying back the individuals noted above—each of whom has played a unique role in the single most remarkable time of my life (16 months wherein I had a baby, survived the first year with that baby, and wrote a book about it)—is to manifest my appreciation in thought, word, and deed from now until the day I expire.

Please consider printed and bound immortality a start—that is, you got your name in a book. It may not have the endurance of a Zip disk or the splash of a billboard but I'm doin' the best I can here.

I'll be in touch as subsequent opportunities for displays of gratitude become apparent.

CONTENTS

Introduction

~

Calculating Interest

I am not one of those women who has always known.

In fact, they amaze me—those women. They fell in love with the idea of babies back when they were barely more than babies themselves. And then they stuck with that notion all the way through childhood, adolescence, college, dating, that first job, that first fiancé, the struggle for stability, the search for a mate, all the way through to that little pink "+" on the home-test kit. And all the while, they knew. This and this alone would complete their journey, make whole their person, lift them to that omnipotent place where choices are clear and decisions never second-guessed.

No. That wasn't me.

I've traveled toward and away from the idea of procreation many hundreds of times since my own birth, never convinced that I was meant to have a baby or that a baby was meant to have me. I waited a good long while—a really, really good long while—for that moment when the light would break across my brain and I would see the clear-cut road through the forest, the one that would lead me happily and unquestioningly to babyland.

That light has never appeared.

And yet, on July 4, after holding my nose with my thumb and forefinger, scrunching my eyes shut and diving into the deep dark hole of unprotected sex for several weeks, I got the news. I was pregnant; I am pregnant, with child, knocked up, in the family way. And there was no turning back, despite the fact that all these unanswered questions were still unanswered.

1. Can I physically handle it?
2. Do I have the patience for the job?
3. Can I still have my career and take care of a baby?
4. Will I be able to sidestep my own neuroses, negativity, and compulsions enough to raise a slightly healthy human being?
5. Do I have enough money?

And those are just the questions that break down into simple sentence structure. This biological-clock stuff really doesn't lend itself to grammar and syntax. It's more like one long anxiety-infested primordial scream that doesn't punctuate easily.

Even a year ago, if you'd asked me that dangerous question: "Do you want a child?" I would have taken a really deep breath and said something like this:

"How do you know I don't have a kid? Can you smell it on me? Is my fear of commitment so palpable that you can actually see it? I don't know! Why are you asking me? What? I can't hear

you. My clock is ticking so loud I'm having trouble deciphering your words. No. No. No. Don't shout. It's no use. This tick is the kind of loud that makes little shake marks all around the hard edges of the sound. It reverberates through my whole body and most likely, past my boundary and into your personal space, for which I apologize but maybe you should just Back off!"

My old college pal Gale asked me the dreaded question not all that long ago. I politely informed her about the loud ticking and she said, "Oh, really? You have that? Hm. Mine's digital. I know it's there but I can't hear it."

Digital would be better because maybe the ticking syndrome doesn't signal an actual want for a kid. Maybe it's just some caveman DNA instructive that we've all grown way beyond. The procreational mandate is over, after all. Breeding now is just for kicks. But, on the other hand, maybe the ticking only happens if your subconscious knows better than you your actual wants and desires—and you really do want a kid. Maybe your deep, inner, untouchable self knows that a kid is just the ticket to tweak the whole structure of the universe and right its corners.

But ticking and biology have not been my only questions. I have not led my life in such a way as to bring me perfectly to this moment. My household is not ideal for family life and that offers up a whole other series of questions such as: What if I die and the kid is left with a father who is too old and too broke to take up the charge? Or what if he dies and leaves us all alone? Or what if I end up resenting them both because their existence has hemmed me into a life of bad writing and long commutes? What if the whole thing suddenly compels me to get married when the only thing of which I have finally become certain is that I never want to do that again?

Maybe I'm just too selfish. But here's the thing: My life has always been all about my career and I never thought it would take this long to get just one rung up the ladder. Professionally, as an actress, as a writer, I'm a nose above nothing. If what I have could even be called a career, it's only because it shows signs of forming and not because the actual hard-core matter that makes for a real career actually exists; finance-wise, stability-wise, opportunity-wise. I'm still at that point where I must make major all-consuming efforts to rise above the masses. And at the ripe old age of almost-not-thirty-something-anymore, there's no time for that kind of cogitation.

About four months ago, the boyfriend said, "People have kids for all the wrong reasons but if everyone spent as much time thinking about it as you do, we'd be extinct."

To which I replied, through a bunch of tears and snot, "See, that's the kind of support I'm looking for."

By the way, it is not lost on me, as I write this, that the questions I am presenting keep coming out in present tense. Even though I am presently tense with child and these things should have been resolved a long time ago.

At least I don't feel like there's a gun to my head anymore. Now that I have actually taken the dive, I no longer have to consider and reconsider the stirring words spoken to me by my gynecologist when I presented my ambivalent self to him and said I just wasn't sure how to answer the baby question.

He said in a strong yet calm voice: Fish or cut bait.

That was a strange thing for a gynecologist to say, I think. On the other hand, though, it was effective. I left his office that day nearly ready to shout, "Get in line boys, the first one to ring the bell wins."

But the fishing advice didn't stop the math—the constant

numbers dancing in my head in syncopation with the ticking: 37 + 9 months = 38 - 9 months + breaking up = 38.5 + recovery = 39.25 (w/ mood-enhancing drugs) + hunting and drug withdrawal = 40 + dating and momentary blissful euphoria whereupon I lose all sense of time and believe that anything is possible + moving logistics = 41.4 + concentrated conception efforts (+ possible fertility experts and earning the money to pay for them) = 42.9 + 9 months = 43.

Or, stay with the boyfriend.

Those equations continued to assault my senses even after I pulled on the waders and tied my flies. The numbers just kept whipping by. This is why you need math. If you're in elementary school and you're reading this and you're a girl, this is why. It's also why you need to follow your heart at least as often as you follow your head because just maybe it would have been smarter to have a baby when you were twenty-seven, when you just couldn't see your way through the nuts and bolts of it. Or maybe smart just isn't what this is all about. But still, I would encourage you to study your math.

There were/are other numbers, too. The boyfriend is fifty-seven. Those calculations are pretty simple. You add twenty to everything and before you work up to anything too tricky, you're dead. That's a problem for me. And it's a hard one because I find that I get mad at him for being fifty-seven and, of course, it's not his fault. It's not like he's changed since I met him. He's always been very consistent chronologically. It's just that as things intensify, facts you knew from the beginning transform—their truth changes. Fifty-seven is really old to be having someone who is zero. He would be fifty-seven and the baby would be zero. That might be too great a distance.

Even without a baby, he—assuming all God's blessings on

both of us—will die first. And then I will be left alone. I don't want to be left. Not like that. Not without warning and so irreversibly. Better to just cut the tie myself, gather up a lot of cats, and get wacky and eccentric in a slow way.

Control issues? Maybe.

There are other things about him that are a challenge, too. For example, he comes to the table with preexisting conditions, such as familial ties that could choke a horse. And there's also the fact that on some days, he seems a bit too fond of the jar, as it were. And on all days, he's got a cash-flow problem. Did I mention he's a great playwright?

When Lonnie and I first got together, I remember telling my friend Rodney about him and Rodney said, "Geez, I hope it works out 'cause he sounds like a catch." It was clear that Rodney was being facetious and I don't want the whole world to walk away with that opinion. There are reasons that I am with Lonnie and there are reasons to consider him a wonderful possible dad. The man is brilliant. He's an artist and a teacher and I've never seen anything like it, the way he gives to his students. He's dangerously charming and looks really good in fine clothing that, as a result of his dangerous charm, he has been able to obtain over the course of his travels. He would also like me to mention his culinary talents and that nine times out of ten, he does the grocery shopping and ten times out of ten he does the dishes.

We can both get nutty and we tend to fight viciously, but mostly I like this life we've set up. I like our house, I like our cats, I like the work we do and the fun we have. And all of it is about to change. Forever.

Sometimes, I can see it all, how it lies before me. And I know that I am going to die. Not now but I will and that's really upsetting because I don't want to die. Not ever. Even when I'm feeling like one lonely raw nerve ending, I want more.

I don't understand why we get invited to this party if we're not going to be allowed to stay. I want to stay. I want to stay and I want to dance all night.

This is no great leap from the baby question. It's all about not being left alone and not really dying and recreating youth. Isn't it? And yet, you can't help but recognize that having a baby is as much a giant step toward the cliff's edge as burying your grandmother. In fact, maybe even more so because it's not just a case of one less person in front of you to block your way—now there's actually someone behind you who could decide to push.

I don't want to be pushed and I don't want to fall and I won't leap. I just really don't want to go. I want to stay at the party. Forever.

Clearly, I am still not one of those women.

But even I can see that there's very little point in asking these questions anymore. What will be will be. I have exerted my last bit of control. I got pregnant. I no longer answer questions. Questions answer themselves.

1. *Can I handle it physically?* I don't know. We'll see.
2. *Do I have the patience for the job?* I don't know. We'll see.
3. *Can I still have my career and take care of a baby?* I don't know. We'll see.
4. *Will I be able to sidestep my own neuroses, negativity, and compulsions enough to raise a slightly healthy human being?* I don't know. We'll see.
5. *Do I have enough money?* I don't know. Hmm.

Start-up Costs

~

Original Sum
(The Debt You're Born With)

December 1 — Friday

I spent $614.96 on my daughter yesterday. She is now officially an American. She has stuff and she is in debt.

Her name is Callie. She's not born yet. She'll show up in March. I'm not suggesting that she has to pay me back right away but eventually . . .

I mean, *I'm* not going to use this stuff and she did make me puke for five months straight so it's not like I haven't already given of myself. Anyway, regardless of whatever payment schedule she decides to arrange, I think it's a good idea to start a tally since eighteen years is a long time to remember. It's always best to keep notes.

QTY/ITEM	CAT	PRICE	TOTAL
1 C&J dressing table— white with drawer	furniture	199.99	
1 McClaren Vogue 2000— Blue Louie	transportation	229.99	
1 Evenflo On-My-Way car seat	transportation	89.99	
1 Snap & Go Car Seat stroller frame	transportation	69.99	
	shipping	25.00	
		$614.96	$614.96

So . . .

I'm doing my shopping at Albee's up on Amsterdam because it's where everyone shops. Albee's doesn't have everything; they just have the stuff they've decided is best, which is good because the research on the many thousands of items I'm told I need is becoming overwhelming and I really don't want to start billing Callie for time yet. Billing for hours at this point seems somewhat subjective and unfair since she isn't here to approve the expense. Again, I want it understood that I'm only charging for those items that are mandatory. Later, when she starts requesting optional items, I'll bill for those. But that will be fair since she will have approved the expenditure.

Here's the rule—I ask this question: Would I be spending this money if the baby didn't exist? Yes? She doesn't get billed. No? The kid owes. It's simple.

Anyway, Agnes, the woman who works at Albee's, just

found out three days ago that her daughter is pregnant and although she's none too amused, she is already deciding which items she'll be purchasing for her grandchild and so, I'm just getting Callie everything that Agnes will be getting for her grandchild. It seems like the most reliable and efficient research I could do.

To tell you the truth, I think Agnes is actually adjusting nicely to her daughter's news. She would just prefer it if she were married. I tried to comfort her by telling her I'm not married either. She smiled a little at that. Her eyes widened and she nodded once to the side. But in the end, I'm not sure she was exactly comforted.

Anyway, about the McClaren 2000—they say it's the Cadillac among the strolling set.

December 2—Saturday

I've decided I should include medical bills. Here's my thinking—I wouldn't be going to the gyno every four weeks if it weren't for Callie. And all those tests and scans—they really are hers.

See, the doctor said, when they found those three fibroids during the second ultrasound, that 50 percent of women have them but they never know it because they're not scanning their uteruses on a regular basis. So there you go, it's that simple—most women don't have these procedures unless they're knocked up. Therefore, it's a Callie expense.

And by the way, I'm only including those things that are not covered by insurance. I'm not looking to make a profit here, just an accurate accounting for future payment—no interest charged.

QTY/ITEM	CAT	PRICE	TOTAL
Urine pregnancy test	education	25.00	
Echography transvaginal	photography	315.00	
Urinalysis w/o microscope	blood & urine	4.00	
Obstetric panel	blood & urine	80.00	
Glucose random	blood & urine	24.95	
BUN	blood & urine	24.95	
HIV	blood & urine	52.00	
Venipuncture	blood & urine	3.00	
Urine culture	blood & urine	45.45	
Acupuncture session	puke control	60.00	
Dermatological visit	cancer panic*	100.00	
Amniocentesis	photography	81.00	
Guide for amniocentesis	?**	10.60	
X ray/Op	photography	212.00	
		$1,037.95	$1,652.91

*Estrogen surge—that mole could have been more than a mole.
** I don't remember meeting this person.

In reviewing medical bills, I have come across a few other early expenses that I consider viable for inclusion.

QTY/ITEM	CAT	PRICE	TOTAL
1 Answer Quick & Simple	education	10.29	
2 Victoria's Secret XXL Tights	fat clothes	24.00	
1 Lamaze weekend	anxiety mgmt.	75.00	

continued on next page

continued from previous page			
1 Breast-feeding class	groceries	15.00	
CP Shades	fat clothes	133.19	
Gatsby's	fat clothes	211.02	
Title Nine Sports	fat clothes	66.90	
		$535.40	$2,188.31

I want to point out something—I am not charging rent and Callie is definitely in my space. I see little difference between what's going on in my body and what goes on in apartment buildings across America. My body is not currently available for my use and/or pleasure and yet, I am not asking for a dime. I just wanted that stated for the record in case anyone is thinking this approach is harsh and/or unfair to the unborn.

It's time for all of us to wake up. We've already raised three generations, at least, who are in serious personal entitlement overdrive. I want Callie to be better than that. I want her to know how to take care of herself. I want her to know how much life costs and what things are worth. I want her to know what she's worth.

I would also like to get some money back.

December 7—Thursday

Just back from the pharmacy—

QTY/ITEM	CAT	PRICE	TOTAL
30 Natafort Tabs	medicine	$13.49	$2,201.80

Seeing as these vitamins are, in fair measure, responsible for the endless gastric distress I have experienced lo these many months—I have *absolutely* no problem billing for them. And, just for the record, I'm picking up the tab on the Tums.

Now, as for the ding in the fender—the other day, Callie's purchases from Albee's arrived while I was out getting a bagel. When I returned home and pulled the Subaru into the garage, I was so startled to see a pile of large boxes covered with pictures of baby heads stacked in my garage that I temporarily misplaced the brake—or my foot—and drove into a ladder neatly stored along the wall (unlike the chaotic pile of baby-head boxes).

I tend to think I will not bill for this, but I do want it recorded. Would I have hit the ladder if I had returned to find my garage as I had left it—full of carefully arranged grown-up toys and absent of baby-head mayhem? I think not. Enough said.

That brings me to the issue of cord banking—that is, the harvesting of the blood (read: stem cells) from the umbilical cord at the moment of birth. This, it seems to me, is a foolish thing not to do. Imagine (GOD FORBID in capital letters) finding yourself in a situation where you need those precious stem cells and realizing that because you didn't grab the cord when you could you are now going to have to stand by and watch the clock as the country is searched for a match. No. I think there's little choice in this matter.

The only question that does remain is this: Who pays?

Now, Callie could obviously benefit from this little storage plan but so could anyone in her genetically linked family, and if she sees it on her bill and gets the slightest bit agitated about this arrangement I've set up . . . well, suffice to say, she could get stingy and that could get ugly.

So—I guess I'll cover the initial $1,050. That covers the collection kit, cord-blood processing, maternal blood testing, and the first year of storage.

The ongoing annual storage fee will be discussed at a future date—possibly when Callie is capable of discussing.

December 15—Friday

New tennis shoes have been purchased long before I really needed new tennis shoes because I found myself hobbled by midday yesterday—swollen ankles, puffy feet. I was walking like my water had already broken. It was pathetic.

The shoes are a size 10.

I've never worn a size 10 in my life. I wear an 8½, maybe a 9. I will bestow these shoes upon young Callie at the moment of her birth though I must say, I hope she does not grow into them. Size 10 is big for a girl. I'm hoping her feet are more petite than that.

By the by, I'm sorry she didn't have a say as to color or style but the shoes were needed now. There was no time to wait.

QTY/ITEM	CAT	PRICE	TOTAL
1 NBM803EEBK	transportation	$84.99	$2,286.79

I trust this is temporary—this 10 thing. Neither Callie nor I need to be buying a new collection of shoes at present.

January 5—Friday

Before the holidays really get away from us, I have a few ob-
servations I would like to put down for the record.

I took it upon myself to drive home to Michigan this Christmas in order to, among other things, bring back my grandfather's cradle. I also wanted to help my mom deal with the real
estate broker and get the basement cleared of forty years of ac-
cumulation.

You see, Mom's moving east. She's going to buy a house
down the street so that Callie will never be tossed off on
strangers or into the arms of by-the-hour hired help.

No. Not for Callie. Callie will be with Gramma.

Now it could be said I'm going to save a bundle in child care
and that may very well be true. But, on the flip side, Callie is
going to benefit tenfold from my mother's grace and generosity
and my good management and planning.

Which brings me to another point. Obviously, there are
enormous costs being incurred as Mom begins the segue from
her old life of living alone in the American Midwest and
workaholicking herself into a seven-day-a-week work style to
her new life in colonial New England as a retiree who will
spend some fair portion of her time caring for her one and only
grandchild. But she has said nothing of these expenses to me
and therefore, I am making no note of them to Callie.

But there is a larger issue at hand here and it has to do with
networking. Bear with me.

While home for the holidays, I spent a good amount of time
with my old pals Cindy, Tammy, and Diane. We go back to single digits. We've known each other a long time. They have

three kids each. They live where we all lived once. Diane actually lives in the house in which she grew up, which (until a recent move by Cindy to a bigger house) was a straight shot out of Cindy's kitchen window. Their kids go to our old schools.

I've lived a very different last twenty years from them but for some inexplicable reason, we can still laugh at the same things. They don't, however, any of them, approve of my plans for the nursery. They wanted to know what colors I'd chosen and how I was planning to decorate. I just kind of looked at them stupid. Then I said, "White. The room is white now and I don't plan to change it."

They looked at me like I was not only insane but also in no small part evil. I tried to explain to them that my house is from the colonial period. It is very simple in design. It wouldn't feel right to gussy up a nursery-type room with that ceiling border ducks-and-balloons wallpaper trim. And to paint the room a soft yellow only to paint it back in a few years seems like a waste on many levels, not the least of which is financial, and that is definitely a cost that would land in Callie's column, and therefore, it should not be incurred until she requests it. So, that's it—the day she says, "Something in a pale yellow, please," we'll hop in the car and make a run to the paint store and not before.

Additionally, it has been my feeling that if you fill a white room with baby-size things, a bed with bars, and a large variety of animals that don't move unless you grab them by the neck and rattle them around while making them talk in funny voices—then that room is going to look like a nursery. And life is proving me out nicely on this point.

Getting to the networking point: Callie made a nice haul over the holidays, particularly when you consider the fact that

she doesn't even live here yet and she really doesn't know anyone. Regardless of those handicaps, the girl had a considerable
number of packages under the tree—not to mention her own
handmade (stuffed to the brim) stocking.

She got: cow shoes; red moccasins; a green velour French
pantsuit; a Stuart Little doll with suitcase and pj's; a fur-
trimmed hat; a bib, bag, and hat with matching duck design; a
train that hooks together magnetically and spells her name;
eight hand-me-down outfits in excellent condition; a pair of
festive socks; a Tanglewood T-shirt; two signed limited-edition
prints (one of a shoe and one of a pacifier); a rubber duckie;
and a pair of overalls.

The room looks like a nursery. Trust me.

And why did she get these things? I don't want to belabor
my input and/or importance here, but it is because I have
amazing friends and that didn't just happen overnight. I
have cultivated these friendships over many years. It took a
lot of living and wrong turns and right choices and I have chosen well.

My friends are successful, smart, caring, generous people,
and Callie is reaping the benefits of those connections. It's
called networking and it's a valuable thing. But—and note this,
loud and clear—I offer these connections to my beloved
daughter free of charge and with a happy heart.

The baby shower is scheduled for January 20.

January 8—Monday

Hangers and vitamins (again).

With a wardrobe like hers you don't think you can use

giant-size wire hangers—do you? No. You need little yellow baby hangers.

QTY/ITEM	CAT	PRICE	TOTAL
1 10PK Hangers	wardrobe maintenance	1.79	
30 Natafort Tabs	medicine	14.79	
		$16.58	$2,303.37

And now, it's time to spend a few moments exploring the price of my good looks and their recent demise. I am currently not very attractive. This is not to say that prior to this physical metamorphosis into human rental unit I was a stone-cold brick shit-house man-killer walking down the street pushing fainted and panting victims from my path. I'm not saying that. But I was good-looking enough to make acting in commercials a fair part of my income. That's just not happening right now.

Because, the truth is, while there are roles for pregnant women on TV, the powers that be do not actually want them to be played by pregnant women. I know this to be a fact because I have, in recent months, been to several of these auditions and the look of horror on the faces of the casting agents as my once bookable frame enters the room has told the story loud and clear.

They do not want a real pregnant woman with her full hips, double chins, funky hair, and flashback blemishes. No. What they want is a model with a pillow.

Suffice to say, my little family is currently doing without

that income. Does that go into the Callie column? No. I'm not going to expense it—it would be completely speculative anyway. But I did want it noted.

January 16 — Tuesday

Legal fees—I'm sorry to have to bring them up but the girl is incurring some legal debt on the way to officially becoming the sole heir to my wee fortune. You see, I have just concluded my first session of estate planning with my lawyer. It will cost several hundred dollars in the end though I have not yet been billed. I will bill Callie once I receive the invoice.

It seems more than fair that she should cover this expense. After all, the whole reason I have finally settled down to do this thing—this writing of my will—is that she needs to have the legal instruments necessary to clean out the tills once the stress of all this finally kills me.

On a related note, I do not enjoy reviewing every possible scenario regarding my demise. It is not how I wish to spend my free time. But that's what we did.

Okay—say I die but Lonnie survives, then she'll be with her father. But say her father and I die together—well, then she'll go with my mother. But what if all three of us go down in flames together? Okay, so now we're up to the tertiary guardians. I haven't figured out the tertiarians yet. Instead of coming up with that answer, I decided to make light of the scenario with my lawyer.

"I guess this means my mom, Lonnie, and I shouldn't travel on planes and trains together. Huh?" I smiled.

"I don't know," my lawyer answered. "Because if you do, chances are you would have taken the baby with you."

Here ends the reading for today.

I still need to call my brother, Randy. I made him the executor of the estate although I haven't asked him yet if he's willing. He'll hold the purse strings, assuming he doesn't mind carrying a purse. He's a numbers guy. He'll be good at this.

Callie, however, will be endlessly annoyed because Randy has a soulless sense of right and wrong. He is never swayed — not by loving kindness, not by human suffering. These things are not at the heart of any given issue for him. Rather it's a matter of the expressed desires of the represented and/or the practical, rational truth as it is borne out by the facts.

That is to say, when my sadly senile grandfather was being cleaned out (of what would be our inheritance) by a crew of money-grubbing gold diggers, Randy always felt it necessary to examine the situation from my grandfather's point of view — regardless of senility. I, on the other hand, was a screaming raving lunatic bent on revenge. In my humble opinion, these people needed to die a slow, painful death chained to the steps of a limestone courthouse being trampled by marauding bands of high-priced lawyers in stilettos. Randy's point, however, was simple; it was my grandfather's choice to be cleaned out and it was his money. There was no doubt we must respect those wishes.

Furthermore, in Randy's opinion, plagues are a simple matter of population control and families are a necessary evil.

He will be the rock of Gibralter in doling out the cash. He will rule by the exact letter of my law as I scratch it out with my last dying breath. I will be dead and still completely in charge. It's a dream come true. I hope he says yes.

On another note, in order to stem the "slightly anemic" reading from my last blood test, I have had to begin ingesting an iron supplement. I did not bill Callie for the first round of supplements as I was feeling generous that day. However, the situation has escalated. I've had to switch to a new type of iron pill since the first kind I tried made me puke into a snowdrift at Riverside and Seventy-fifth. This time, I'm billing.

QTY/ITEM	CAT	PRICE	TOTAL
10 Niferex 150	anemic patrol	$2.50	$2,305.87

January 23 — Tuesday

Dear Callie,

Sorry about the pushing and shoving this morning but one of the doctors suggested last week that maybe you weren't as big as you're supposed to be. Turns out that's not really true, you're fine. But we needed to take a look. The pushing and shoving was the camera that put you on TV. By the way, it wasn't polite the way you stuck out your tongue. I did appreciate the thumbs-up move though.

So you're on the small side of normal. I'm surprised considering my—our—genetics. Your father says you must come from the petite side of my line. That may be but I don't know where those people are. Perhaps they're still in Norway as they were too weak to make the trip.

Anyway, I was very happy to see you and hear that you're fine and that those fibroids I grew aren't really in your way. I've been a little worried this last week as I waited for this test — ever since it was suggested that you might be a little small.

Actually, there have been a lot of things going on in the last few days that have had me on a bit of an emotional roller coaster and most of it has had to do with you.

For example, your shower was a few days ago. I don't know how you felt about it but I found it a little overwhelming. We were surrounded by a hoard of folks who had gathered simply to celebrate you and give us stuff. There were so many people from so many different parts of my life. I could have lined them up to mark off the years. And I was so proud of them, the way they mingled so nicely with each other. And the actual shower, fully catered and very elegant, was really more of a storm. The whole thing was great but there comes a point when you just don't know what else to say because the generosity and care has been so complete and so one-sided. I ran out of words.

Your grandmother was there, too. She brought you the complete Winnie the Pooh collection in big letters since your eyes won't be fully developed for a good long while. She's moving here all the way from Michigan, where people in my family have been living and dying for several generations. You'll be the first East Coaster.

Your grandmother is terrified. She's leaving everything she's known for six-and-a-half decades because the notion of watching you grow up makes it worth that to her. It's given her the gumption to rise to the occasion.

And then there's Sophie. She's one of our cats. We have four. Sophie is the second oldest. She is small and orange and is a love sponge who lives to ride around on my shoulder. But she's always been sick, too, intestinal troubles that make her very thin and the recipient of cortisone shots every two months. Well, she had her vet visit yesterday and I knew the report would not be good. I know when she's slipping. I can see it in her eyes and I knew we'd been losing ground for several weeks now. The doc confirmed it. She's lost two pounds in the last two months. She weighs four-and-a-half pounds now. I told the doc my suspicions; I think there's cancer. I think the cortisone has finally done all its good and now it's doing some bad. The doc said he suspected I was right. I told him I don't want to do anything. Her appetite is good, ravenous to be exact, and she still likes to ride on my shoulder and she purrs when she's in a comfortable nook of my arm. If this is how she is going to slip away then it's as much as I can ask for. I don't want her poked and cut and caged just to find out she's dying. Better she should just go in her own way. I also mentioned to the doctor another of my theories. It seems as though Sophie is fading away in exact precision with you being born. I expected him to chuckle and wave me off but he didn't.

So I said, "It's as if she knows I can't take care of both of them at once and she's bowing out. I think she's intuitive like that."

The doc's lip lifted in a half smile and he said, "I think that's possible."

I want you to meet Sophie. I hope you will at least pass each other on the road.

You see how it's been a bit of a bumpy ride. These are not the financials, Miss. These are the real tallies, the true payments and the actual price tags. This is the stuff on which you cannot collect and you can never pay back. You simply give thanks or endure with as much grace as you can muster.

January 28 — Sunday

The following is a full listing of goods procured by way of the baby storm. Suffice to say, it was a nice haul.

Callie got: 7 pairs of socks, 3 gowns, 17 onesies, 8 T-shirts, 7 sleepers, 9 dress-up outfits, 8 hats, 4 pair of mitts, 1 pair of dress shoes, 1 pair of tennis shoes, 3 pair of booties, a diaper hamper, 5 large hooded towels, 3 small hooded towels, 9 washcloths, a frog-headed raincoat, 14 books and the Beatrix Potter box set, 2 CDs (1 Mozart, 1 Pat the Bunny), a picture frame, a Pat the Bunny videotape, a bath tub/bath seat combo tub, hand refresher lotion, a musical bouncy seat, a fork and spoon set (zoo animal pattern), 2 silver spoons, a cat and the fiddle night-light, a sweat suit, 2 receiving blankets, a fleece roll-up blanket, a stuffed hammer, a Graco Ultraclear monitor, an Irish wool cardigan, a pink barrette, a decorative ice skate, a fleece bunting, a red satin Chinese cape with hood, a dozen diapers, a $50.00 gift certificate to Albee's, a Lamaze rattle toy, a crib sheet, wooden building blocks, an Evenflo Outbound Frame Carrier, a pocket-size photo album, a 4-piece crib bedding set (Classic Pooh design), an automatic swing, the Avent Newborn starter set of bottles, a tin drinking cup, a silver and rhinestone shoe charm, 3 bibs, a stuffed worm, a diaper bag, a wrist rattle, 2 pair of long underwear, a homeopathy medical kit, homeopathic diaper ointment, a handmade smocked dress, the Medela mini-electric breast pump, and a stuffed pig.

I have written twenty-five thank-you notes thus far. It's the way I was raised and it's the way Callie will be raised. Thank-you notes are the foundation of civilization and, plain put, just a darn good idea. I'm happy to do it, don't begrudge it, even made my own stationery with my nifty new digital camera. But it's clear that the cost of postage and envelopes (which I got on sale) lies squarely on the petite shoulders of the Divine Miss C.

QTY/ITEM	CAT	PRICE	TOTAL
2 25-pack envelopes @ $7.13	civility	14.26	
36 Stamps @ $.34	good breeding	12.24	
		$26.50	$2,332.37

On another note, my OB-GYN recently explained to me that pregnancy is a form of psychosis. I know this is true if for no other reason than I found his observation comforting.

I also have watched myself in the last week, since the baby storm, fall into a rather obsessive cycle of shopping and spending. It's as if the acquisitions of the storm threw the switch and now all I can do is continue to acquire until there is no room left in the house for any of us. I swear all I'm doing is gathering up those odds and ends, those last-minute necessities. But, somehow, the list doesn't seem to be getting any shorter. I just keep picking up and picking up and picking up.

Although I could justify billing it all to Callie as she is the reason for my newfound psychosis, I am opting to wait until I have an official diagnosis. Until such time, I will help cover the cost.

I had a bad bout this weekend. First, I went to Sears.

QTY/ITEM	CAT	PRICE	TOTAL
1 fleece stroller blanket	bedding	11.99	
1 Cuddly crib blanket	bedding	11.99	
2 2-pack gowns @ 11.99	newborn wear	23.98	
3 3-pack lap pads @ 4.49	protection	13.47	
1 2-pack receiving blankets	bedding	9.99	
1 Crib sheet	bedding	10.99	
1 Eeyore play pal	visual stimulation	(5.49)	Complimentary
		82.41	
Tax	civics	4.12	
		$86.53	$2,418.90

Then I went to Filene's.

QTY/ITEM	CAT	PRICE	TOTAL
1 Plush musical pink elephant	audio/visual	(22.00)	Complimentary
1 Mitt with rattles	safety/stimulation	8.00	
1 Plush crib mobile	visual stimulation	(16.00)	Complimentary
1 Fleece bunting	outdoor wear	6.93	
		14.93	
Tax	citizenship	1.16	
		$16.09	$2,434.99

Then I went to another department in Filene's.

QTY/ITEM	CAT	PRICE	TOTAL
1 Underwire Nursing Bra (30% off)	support	$17.07	
			$2,452.06

I stopped at CVS on the way home.

QTY/ITEM	CAT	PRICE	TOTAL
1 Nursing pads	appearances	3.99	
1 Desitin cream	pain relief	5.39	
1 Nursery care set	medical	6.99	
1 Lansinoh cream	my nerves	9.49	
1 KDI underarm thermometer	medical	12.39	
1 48-pack Pampers Premium	hygiene	9.49	
1 CVS baby wipes	hygiene	2.99	
1 Shout liquid	future wardrobe maintenance	3.39	
		54.12	
Tax	social responsibility	1.69	
		$55.81	$2,507.87

Also, I needed more iron supplements and I was forced to buy a box of one hundred.

QTY/ITEM	CAT	PRICE	TOTAL
100 Niferex 150	anemic patrol	$43.22	$2,551.09

January 29 — Monday

Today, I went to Ames.

QTY/ITEM	CAT	PRICE	TOTAL
1 10-pack hangers trays	wardrobe maintenance	1.79	
1 Crib pad	protection	5.99	
1 3-pack organizing trays	nursery maintenance	1.50	
1 Receiving blanket	bedding	6.99	
		16.27	
Tax		.92	
		$17.19	$2,568.28

January 30 — Tuesday

Fair is fair.

I was going to go to the movies last night, see one of the last films I will see for years if I am to believe my informants from the other side. I was just about to get off the couch and put clothes on when Callie starting choreographing a new piece. It was a percussive thing with big rolls and lots of lunges. It was fascinating and it kept me occupied for a good hour, long enough to opt out of the movie.

So, since I decided to stay home and watch my stomach rather than going out to watch a movie, I feel it's only fair that Callie be credited with the savings.

QTY/ITEM	CAT	PRICE	TOTAL
1 Movie ticket	entertainment	8.00	
1 Small popcorn	refreshment	2.75	
1 Small soda	refreshment	2.25	
		+ $13.00	($13.00)

January 31 — Wednesday

Okay. Just a few more things . . . and one last stop at Albee's because I have to use up that gift certificate anyway.

QTY/ITEM	CAT	PRICE	TOTAL
1 Boppy nursing pillow	dining room furniture	29.99	
2 12-pack gerber diapers	environmental protection	43.98	
1 Baby Bjorn bib	wardrobe maintenance	7.99	
2 12-pack outlet covers	safety and welfare (OSHA)	6.98	
1 Stroller rain cover	baby maintenance	14.99	
		103.93	
Tax		8.57	
		112.50	
	Gift Certificate	– 50.00	
		$62.50	$2,630.78

February 2 — Friday

I would like to take a moment to focus on the needs of the environment.

I have spent a considerable amount of time in recent weeks trying to unearth a cloth diaper service anywhere near me. I'm willing to pay cash dollars to have a truck visit once a week to pick up and deliver dirty and clean. I'm even willing to cover the cost myself even though this is obviously Callie's s**t.

But there just isn't one. Nowhere near here; California might be the closest locale with such a service. And when I ask my friends they look at me with this annoying "just wait 'til you have children, dear" look. Obviously, there is no longer a viable market for the dedicated professional diaper cleaner — another skilled laborer up s**t's creek without a paddle.

I'm not trying to be some kind of militant, subdivision-burning environmentalist here. I just want to make an effort to use old-fashioned cloth diapers when I'm at home. I'll take the Pampers on the road just like I'll take any damn drug they offer during delivery. This is the '00s (read: uh-oh's) and I am a child of them. But there comes a point when we're talking just plain old-fashioned irresponsibility and slothfulness. Just as I am not snorting a lot of heroin or smoking crack cocaine right now even though I will take the delivery-friendly drugs — I do not wish to use disposable diapers on those days when we'll be home all day and perfectly able to toss the offending cotton into the Maytag. There are moments for convenience (disposable) and there are moments for the norm (cloth). Without the cloth moments, the disposable moments are no longer considered the convenience. If one never uses cloth then disposable becomes the norm and we're left without a convenience. Convenience abhors a vacuum. Soon we will have created an even easier and more effortless route that will, without question, be tenfold worse for the environment.

I think that's clear even if you don't. Perhaps this set of ratios will help to clarify:

Any and all drugs during delivery:
Heroin and crack now

=

Disposables when necessary due to location/schedule:
Disposables all the time

I can't tell you the crap I'm taking for this view, the rolling eyes, the smirks, the furrowed brows. Clearly, I'm going to have to arm myself. I know there are some staggering statistics about the percentage of our landfills that are taken up by disposable diapers; I should have them in my hip pocket so that I can brandish them like a sword when my faux socially responsible contemporaries begin their dance of dismissal.

Cloth diapers are not easy to find. Diaper covers are even tougher. Further, cloth diapers at Albee's are not displayed according to size, they're displayed according to weave. I believe that this suggests they are not being purchased or marketed as diapers at all but rather as cleanup, burp-up, buff-up towels. As I said, there's no market—even in the hippest of surroundings.

In the end, I discovered www.greenmountaindiapers.com. They sell diaper covers. I purchased three.

QTY/ITEM	CAT	PRICE	TOTAL
2 Bummi Super Whisper/white	environmental protection	17.90	
1 Bummi Super Whisper/Noah's Ark	environmental protection	8.50	
		26.40	
	standard shipping	6.75	
		$33.15	$2,663.93

I hope Callie sees the humor in having a biblical flood on her diapers as I don't think diaper covers are returnable.

February 3 — Saturday

QTY/ITEM	CAT	PRICE	TOTAL
1 6-Gal Periwinkle Trash Can*	sanitation	$4.80	$2,668.73

*Diaper pail

February 23 — Friday

QTY/ITEM	CAT	PRICE	TOTAL
30 Natafort tabs	medicine (vitamins)	$14.79	$2,683.52

The receipt for the above-mentioned vitamins is dated February 7. I am somewhat behind. I am somewhat asleep. We have already discussed the fair-market value regarding the demise of my good looks. We have not, however, dissected, itemized, and broken out the sad loss of my intellect, the value of my brain, the dollars and cents of my lost sense.

I sleep most of the time now. I don't want to. I want to write an opus and sometimes I think that I am. But then I wake up and realize I was not writing an opus. I was sleeping. Not unlike the years and years of my midchildhood when I could have sworn I was getting up and out of bed, walking down the hall, sitting on the toilet, and peeing — only to quickly realize that I, in fact, was still asleep and wetting the bed. I have heard that bed-wetting is genetic. I hope Callie doesn't do it. It makes for so much trauma — so many late-night excuses for leaving the slumber party.

The train. I'm having trouble with the train. Of thought, that is.

Doc says pregnancy is psychosis. Yes. He's got a point.

Callie is scheduled to arrive in 2.5 weeks. I would like to say I still believe she will be early — put an end to this madness, this sliding down into a sea of fatigue and confusion. But I don't think so. I think she's gonna stay right where she is and continue to kick the bejesus out of my right rib until she's good and ready and more than a little late.

Did I mention the cats? There are cats just showing up suddenly. Cats I don't know, and I think they're all pregnant. One appeared in the basement—actually broke into the house somehow. We're calling her Dolly. One is living in the barn—call him James. There's some kind of sign or invisible feline symbol hanging over the house. It says "Ya'll come!" As I said, some or all may be pregnant. Kittens. Litters. Everybody's doin' it.

Turn back! Save yourself! Don't come near this house! It's fertile, I tell you. Fertile and psychotic. I don't know—is it Sophie? Is it Callie? I am living in a never-never land between life, death, and creation. Everything is moving toward transition—toward birth, toward death, toward the loss of all logical thought.

No more feeding the huddled and furry masses.

February 28 — Wednesday

Oh.

My.

God.

This is me—after my nap. It's five days later. I could have sworn I was getting right back to this. Yet, it appears that nearly a week has passed and I've done nothing. Truly. Nothing. Okay. Oprah. I've done Oprah. I love Oprah. Oprah rocks. Oprah could be president. I would vote for her.

This is me without work, without the manic runaround that

is my work-a-day life. This is me on maternity leave—four months, fully paid. I should be devouring the world and setting it on fire. Nothing but time—and an extra forty pounds of estrogen—but never mind.

Time is evolving. It's twisting and turning and telling me it is different things to different people, all things to all people. It can't be pinned down and it will pass as it cares to. I have no control.

Things are disappearing. Things like my sense of productivity, my work ethic, my overwhelming need to "do" in order to prove that I am. One might suggest this could be the greatest gift a child could give—a sense of one's own self-worth that does not come nailed down to the accomplishments of any given week. But such is not the case. I am not free of the syndrome, the guilt, the brutal self-flagellation—just the ability to feed the monster.

'Cause I'm busy, sleeping . . . and watching a little Oprah.

March 1 — Thursday

QTY/ITEM	CAT	PRICE	TOTAL
1 Carb monoxide detector	protection/guilt prevention	58.98	
1 2-pack 9V alkaline battery	fire alarm backup	5.10	
		$64.08	$2,747.60

I've never felt an overwhelming need to protect myself from that silent killer, that invisible fog, that ghastly gas—carbon monoxide. That particular molecule has never scared me. Call me stupid but I've traveled thus far, through this life, unencumbered with that particular concern. But what if it took Miss Callie? And I could have stopped it? That much loss and that much guilt stirred together in one pot—now that's scary. So, carbon monoxide is now being monitored and scrutinized. It is not allowed in this house—not alone, not on the back of some unidentified cat—it simply cannot come in. It's not a consideration, not a risk I can take. And that's gonna cost the girl because those detectors are way more pricey that I thought.

However, due to a collision of forces this week, I find that I don't feel at all badly about billing her for that. I have just learned through my deeply informative one-time-only breast-feeding class that my opting to go the au naturel route is gonna save the kid a bundle. Turns out store-bought formula can run five bucks a day! You do the math. I let Callie drain me dry and as a result she banks $150 a month. That's more than a little gas money, my friend. A round of diapers for everyone!

March 2—Friday

Did I mention there was another baby shower? This one was an ambush. The girls from the village just suddenly appeared. They filled up my kitchen with casseroles, presents, and themselves. It's a small town and events like this choke me up a bit after twenty years of living in the city. It makes me think I'm living in a Thornton Wilder play. But then again, at this particular moment in time, paint drying and grass growing also make me cry.

Regardless of tears and, more to the point, the babe-in-waiting chalked up a nice new batch of complimentary items.

She got: a bundle of stuffed rattles, 2 containers of Just for Me Flushable Moist Wipes, a white receiving gown for greeting visitors and admirers, a 68-pack of unisex Cotton-tail disposable diapers featuring illustrations by Beatrix Potter, a stuffed bear disguised as a rabbit, an orange playsuit with a matching eared hat, a Baby Bee starter kit of bath products, 4 plastic lidded bowls, one tube of Desitin ointment, a Winnie-the-Pooh washcloth, a black-and-white rattle, one stuffed Beanie Baby snake, a book with a stuffed dog, one pair of tricolored moccasins, a Baby Bjorn plastic bib, one receiving blanket, a box of bottle inserts, a pacifier, one bottle of Baby Magic baby bath, and a bar of soap.

March 3 — Saturday

I have a little project for you. Choose a twenty-four-hour period, any one you like, and then count how many times you bend at the waist. You also might want to keep notes as to why you are bending and the relative importance of each bend. For example, bending over to pick up a napkin might not ultimately be that important or valuable. However, bending over to pick up your pants after having used the facilities — well, that might rank a little higher, especially when away from home. Assign each bend with a monetary value, then add up the numbers and figure out the worth of your waist — on a daily basis.

Now acknowledge that I no longer have one and tell me you're sorry for my loss.

I do not bend anymore. Something happened in the last week or so—maximum capacity perhaps. I now am absolutely nothing more than a vessel, a container, Tupperware for the very, very young. I lay on the ground like our friends the earless seals, slap my hands and feet together, and bark.

Please note that I will not bill Callie for my waist. But I miss it, am having trouble living without it, and needed to talk about it.

Mom gets in tomorrow. She's hauling her Honda across Canada even as we speak. She retired on Wednesday, turned sixty-five on Thursday, and started driving across the country today, Saturday. After spending the better part of the last twenty years hunkered down in recovery from a husband-gone-a-walking and the harsh realities of life in general, she has caught up to the rest of us in one short week.

See, now that makes me cry, too.

Once Mom arrives, all bets are off. Come Monday, I will walk up every stair, every steep hill, take long rides in bumpy trucks, and have sex with any man who offers. I will make it very difficult for this child not to appear.

I need to purchase a rocking chair. I forgot the rocking chair. Perhaps I am not as prepared as I thought.

March 7—Wednesday

Puked this morning.

Don't know what that was about but it sent me right back to bed and I've made a few decisions. The most important of which is this: I'm staying here until the tiny chick shows up. No more folding baby clothes, no more running errands, no more politely returning every phone call that comes in. And no more shopping. (However, I will keep in place my plan for stair-climbing-, hill-walking-, truck-riding-, sex-having-induction methods.)

So, here ends the prenatal spending. I am putting my foot down — swollen and grotesque as it may be. There will be no more until Miss Callie has arrived.

I am too sick, too tired, and too confused. I could get hurt at the mall.

I'll be in bed eating bonbons, watching Oprah, and petting the cats. I'll be holding Sophie close as it appears she is bound and determined to be present and accounted for at the arrival of the newest kitten. (I hope she is not disappointed by the lack of fur and tail, and I guess, in accordance with that, I hope there is a lack of fur and tail.)

By the way, Dad found an old rocking chair at a flea market back in Michigan. He and the Mrs. are refinishing and re-upholstering and he'll deliver it himself, thus saving his granddaughter all expenses including shipping.

The nursery is ready and on standby.

Credits: $13.00
Disbursements: $2,747.60

The First
Fiscal Quarter

~

Postpartum Recession

Subj: *Could It Be?*
Date: *3/13 (Tuesday)*

It's 2:30 in the A.M.

To the many of you who have been so fabulous as to be calling and E-ing (and for those of you who have been so fabulous as to not) in regards to whether or not this child of mine has made her appearance or not — I am E-ing to let you know that it appears we are finally on our way to the hospital.

From here, it looks like a good idea to bring the laptop and keep you all thoroughly up to date on the progress. However, even I can tell that that may be one of those ideas whose glory fades in the heat of the moment, as it were.

I will be in touch.

Love,

Betsy

Subj: *uhhh . . . well . . .*
Date: *3/13*

Okay—it's ten hours later.

The kid has pulled some impressive maneuvers but it seems she is reluctant to make this a quick and easy ride.

Please, go about your business and don't mind us.

We have now returned home, where we are continuing to explore the true meaning behind those classic lyrics "twist and shout"—and having a wonderful time.

What can I tell you? So far, this has been really, really fun. (Please read with as little emotion as possible.)

More as more is available.

Betsy

Subj: *and furthermore . . .*
Date: *3/13*

Only because so many of you seem to be enjoying the blow by blow—as it were—here is the latest. After a day of contractions and retractions, that irreversible tidal wave has hit and so we are heading back to the hospital—although now I am a seasoned veteran and know I do not need to rush. Therefore, I will have a little dinner, fix my hair, and be on my way. The doc will check us out and then . . . we'll see.

Once again, I will be in touch.

Love,

Betsy

March 14—Wednesday

Labor means work. That's what the doc keeps saying.

Labor means delirium. That's what I am saying. I think. I

hear it but I don't have proof it's been spoken aloud, not like the conversation I can hear around me.

Conversation between Dad and Lonnie—I am in and out of coherent—a night of morphine, a shot of Stadol—the pain keeps getting worse and the baby's not dropping and I'm not dilated and when I rise to the surface and see into my mother's eyes, the doctor's eyes—they are not light—they are worried. This is not going well.

I hear Dad's voice—I rise. He is talking to Lonnie. His sound, it's nostalgic. I think, he's scared . . .

"You ever play ball with her?"

"Baseball?" Lonnie asks.

"Yeah," Dad answers.

"Sure. We've thrown the ball around."

Dad chuckles. I know what is coming. He's going to brag about my arm. "I used to hate playing catch with her because it hurt to catch the ball."

Lonnie is holding my hand as a contraction rears its head, comes charging through me like a train, its blinding headlights breaking open the night.

"Yeah," Lonnie says, "I know I'm not supposed to say this but she—"

"—throws like a boy." I spit it out between deep breaths.

Dad and Lonnie, I see them smile through the haze.

"Yeah, she has babies like a boy, too."

And now I'm not so worried. Dad is back in form. Got one in. And a good one. Funny.

"You try it," I growl and now I sink again—narcoticked out.

And then it is hours later and the drugs are improved . . . intrathecal . . . shot in the spine . . . bent over during contractions . . . can't move . . . needle in my spine . . . nails into metal gripping and so afraid. But then there is an easing up, a relief. Fully feeling the strength of the contraction, the pressure, but the pain is somehow somewhere else.

The bed rises and falls, transforms into a chair. I am in a sitting position, hands grabbing onto handles at my side. I feel like I am the commander of *Star Trek's Enterprise*—if Sharon Stone were the commander.

I am not yet at 10—8.5.

It's been twenty-four hours since my water broke. It's time. The baby needs to come. There is gravity in the air. I need to pee. I cannot pee. I am shaking and bleeding on the floor when I try to walk. Kay, the midwife, reapplies Chapstick and tells me I'm doing fine. I laugh at her, call her Suzy Chaffee, wonder what kind of commercial Chapstick could make out of this.

Finally, it's been twenty-seven hours since my water broke and I am at 10. It's time for the big push.

Mom is at my head. I can feel her touch even when her skin is inches from mine. And I can hear my Dad's voice as he calls out encouragement, low and steady. He has found himself a wheelchair and is scooting back and forth over the threshold of the door. This is a whole lot of view for him. He hasn't seen this much of me since I was Callie's age. But he's here and my parents have spent more time together in the last day than they have in the last twenty years. No new spouses and no other children—just my mom, my dad, and me—it's been a long time. And of course, Dr. Schnurr and Kay (who I think has perhaps saved my life today with her steady soul) and the nurses and whoever else might happen to pass by.

Lonnie is standing at my feet gripping the other end of the

towel I pull on with all my might during each contraction. I must be careful not to let go too quickly once the contraction eases or he will quite literally go flying into the cinder-block wall behind him. And this ain't like no tug-of-war he ever played with the Jesuits back in Catholic school.

It's getting ugly.

And it gets worse before it gets better. Much worse. I scream at my mother not to touch me. I shout at a nurse I don't recognize. My head spins in circles. I puke pea soup.

It's been twenty-nine hours since my water broke. It's past time. The baby really needs to come.

And finally — she does.

Subj: Introducing . . .
Date: 3/15 (Thursday)

Callie
March 14
11:08 P.M.
6 lbs. 14 oz.
21 inches

Please accept our apologies for the delay in this update to our previous transmissions. Trust me, I never thought it would take this long.

But she is way cute so her hesitancy is forgiven.

Thanks for all your support. I will be in touch when I am a little more recovered.

Love,

Betsy

March 15 — Thursday

QTY/ITEM	CAT	PRICE	TOTAL
30 Natafort tabs	medicine (vitamins)	$15.99	$2,763.59

March 16 — Friday

QTY/ITEM	CAT	PRICE	TOTAL
1 Growing family— photos	"once in a lifetime" file	56.03	
1 Always overnight	hemorrhaging	3.49	
1 Motrin IB	pain	8.89	
1 4-pack alk batteries	digital photos	5.69	
1 Isopryl alcohol	cord maintenance	.99	
1 Colace stool softener	'nuf said	9.64	
		$84.73	$2,848.32

March 17 — Saturday

I cry in the shower. I just keep shaving my legs. I know it's hormonal. Sort of. I can see her face even when I'm staring into the water pouring down on me. I look into Callie's little face whether it's in front of me or floating like a vision as when

I am in the shower and I just start to cry—the body slam of
genuine untouched sweetness, so pure. It doesn't belong here.

March 18—Sunday

Ice packs on my tits and I'm starting to see it—the full-blown
damage of it all—the collateral damage. And it has no price.

March 19—Monday

QTY/ITEM	CAT	PRICE	TOTAL
1 Doctor visit	inexperience	15.00	
1 Tube Vaseline petroleum jelly	lube job— backend	2.53	
		$17.53	$2,865.85

Found an old receipt—March 4. The last bottle of Tums I
will ever buy. As I have not charged Callie for many of the
previous seventy-nine bottles, I feel justified in billing for this
final batch.

QTY/ITEM	CAT	PRICE	TOTAL
1 Tums	final solution	$4.79	$2,870.64

March 20 — Tuesday

QTY/ITEM	CAT	PRICE	TOTAL
1 14 Ibuprofen tab 600 MG	professional pain	$4.06	$2,874.70

March 21 — Wednesday

My daughter was born one week ago today. It was really, really hard.

Without question, it was the scariest thing I have ever experienced. I feel that perhaps it has come down to me to blow the lid off this situation. Ever since I got pregnant, it seems to me that other women — who have themselves been pregnant, who have themselves always spoken so highly of "that magical time" — once I was pregnant — in the club, as it were — began to whisper, slowly at first and then with more regularity. They hated being pregnant, they told me. More and more of them would talk to me when no one was looking — they couldn't wait for it to end, they would say. They quietly mumbled their war stories, shutting up when young girls passed. They admitted horrible things about their feelings toward the alien within.

And now, now that I have faced the ultimate terror and given birth to this child — forced a bowling ball through the eye of a needle — now those same women in response to the horror story I tell them, they are saying things like, "Yeah, you never know how much to tell someone."

WHAT!?

They knew! They knew all along and they kept it to themselves. I'm telling you, this is some kind of twisted Darwinistic attempt at keeping the species on an ever upward march—keep those babies coming!

"For God's sake," screams the Genome, "don't tell the women—they'll never breed again!" And the women—they obligingly step to that DNA drum, keeping their mouths shut waiting for the next sucker to walk the plank.

"Oh, but you forget all of it."

"Oh, but it's so worth it!"

"Oh, but look what you get."

That is not the point! This lying must stop and I am here to do it. Pregnancy absolutely sucks. And labor and delivery sucks even more.

I did not have a good time.

And yet, now, I just weep. She is truly beautiful. I cry when I look at her. Also, I cry when I look at toast and dust—but I cry more when I look at her because she's so lovely.

Dear Callie,

I just weep. I'll sit—in my oh-so-careful way as I try to slow the pain of impact as butt meets chair—I'll just sit with you in my arms. We've just had a great success of it—you at my breast—and you are gazing up at me, or something close to me, it's hard to tell where you're focused. But this peace sits so softly upon your face that I begin to weep. I do not make noise because I do not want your father or your grandmother to hear me because this is not postpartum depression and it's not the baby blues. Tears are not streaming down my face be-

cause of the fear that I feel, which I do, or the anxious-
ness that I feel, which I do—the tears are from a place
somewhere outside of me that recognizes sheer beauty
and absolute trust when it sees it. Those that watch from
that place recognize when something too good and too
pure and too soft has landed among us and the watchers
send tears to fall from whatever pair of eyes gaze most
nearly upon that sweetness.

You make me weep in a way that doesn't work out in
words. Maybe there is a tone or a rhythmic thumping
that drives to the heart of this thing that I am feeling,
something at least as old as the caveman—a leap and a
howl or a stick and a rock—something in those tools
might express the feeling that floods when the tears start
to fall, but I don't know what.

So, it appears, I'm being transformed by the tiniest of
people. You have wrecked me, destroyed my perfect
frank glibness. And you threaten to rob me of my desire
to care about any number of things—work, play, money.
And so what is the billable cost of that?

How do I charge you for stealing my want to do anything but stare at you?

If you have nicked my desire to care about cash and
career then how can I care enough to want to charge you
for the theft?

You leave me in a conundrum.

Perhaps I will return to my senses by late spring and
understand again that this is a fair and equitable deal
and it's important that I teach you the value of things.
So, I will continue to total the tally on the chance that
one day I will see some part of my sense again. On the

chance that, one day, you will open up your lovely little long-fingered hands and let me take just a peek at my soul, which it would appear, you now own.

Pardon me for rambling, but I'm just recovering from being split like an amoeba.

March 22 — Thursday

I must consider some kind of credit program. It has come to my attention that I am not spending any money. I am not spending any money because I cannot figure out how to leave the house. If I cannot leave the house, I cannot select objects that I would like to purchase and, therefore, I cannot hand my money over to other people for them to keep so that I might depart with said objects.

It's Callie's fault. She is the reason I have forgotten how to leave the house. I get scared at the thought, at the notion of tipping this precarious little construct we have here that doesn't really even look like a construct but it's all I have so I'm clinging to it like Kate Winslet to the rail of the *Titanic.*

I am a prisoner and Callie is the warden. So why a credit program, you ask? Must I pay the warden for keeping me from the mall? What is this, the Stockholm syndrome — or was it Helsinki? My captor, my savior. I must dwell on this. I am unsure of the soundness of my theory as I am working at diminished capacity. This could be foolish babble but I swear I can hear it, garbled in her crying maybe, but I swear she is calling me Prisoner 75109 — or is that just the soundtrack from *Les Mis* conjured because she looks like such a waif?

If my mother were not here, I would not survive this. I look at Callie, I cry. I look at my mother, I cry. And it's from the same thing. It's the generosity of love spilling over and staining everything it touches. This is all very messy; I cannot "Shout" it out, and it makes my skin crawl a little to type it out loud.

> *Note to self: Consider getting the cleaning lady in once a week rather than every two weeks. Bill extra visits to child.*

March 25 — Sunday

I'm in a very surreal place that has no outdoors and very few other people and my breasts are worshipped like some kind of mythological Goddess and time doesn't exist. I wonder if the people out there have noticed that I've gone missing. I wonder if they wonder about me, miss me.

Oh, God. I wonder if they're still there . . .

March 26 — Monday

Everything sounds like a baby crying. Those first choking barks that signal the end of my time and the start of another feeding or another rocking or another walk on swaying sea legs — I find I have come to fear that sound. Sometimes, I look at her sleeping so peacefully and I find that I fear her, what she will ask of me, whether I will be strong enough to hold up under the request.

March 27 — Tuesday

I put Callie in the back seat. I put my mom in next to her, armed with a quarter-dozen blankets aimed at warming the baby and hiding my guilt.

One of the blankets just arrived today—another gift. They will not stop coming, the gifts. No matter what I do, boxes arrive and I always owe at least six thank-you notes. I am running low on gracious charm and it's so tiring to continually write sweet thank-yous that do not somehow reveal my cracking psyche.

But never mind.

I bury my baby and mother in blankets because she's not supposed to be out until it's at least 60 degrees. (The baby, not my mom. My mom can go out whenever she feels like it, at any temperature. That's been the case ever since I can remember. Mom has been allowed to make those choices for herself.) Sixty degrees and it's not even close 'cause this is the longest winter since I don't know when and the fucking snow just keeps coming down and it's just never going to end—

But never mind.

I get behind the wheel and peel out from the driveway because I just have to. I just have to go. I have to get out and see roads and signs and stores and people and any little suggestion that the world is continuing to spin despite my absence.

Perhaps I am a scoshe depressed.

I drive from store to store and I buy things. At the pharmacy I walk up and down the aisles. I look at all the people and they don't seem to notice that I have escaped. They act like everything is normal. I act like I am just here for the graham crackers and chocolate milk, which nearly gives me away as I ask for them at the counter, remembering as I speak that pharmacies don't carry graham crackers and chocolate milk.

So I buy some infant Tylenol instead since the doctor said we should have some on hand after he stuck her with that needle yesterday to guard her from Hepatitis B and I appreciate that but it hurt her and she howled like she was pissed off in a new kind of way that she never imagined possible and like she was really in pain and I had let it happen and I cried, too. But I cried more quietly.

QTY/ITEM	CAT	PRICE	TOTAL
1 Tylenol Inf/Susp 15ML ch	temp prevention	$5.49	$2,880.19

At every stop I pick up some sugar. I'm consuming approximately one family-size bag of jelly beans and/or spice drops a day. My mother is my main supplier but I take advantage of this spree and slip a little something in my bag at each stop. I pay for it, I'm not suggesting thievery, I just don't need the whole world in my business and if I need a little sugar right now to get my through then so be it. I'm not handling this well. There's a pit in my stomach and I can't seem to fill it.

We go to Ames. I let the motor run so the car stays warm. I smile at my mom, crunched into the back seat. I am stabbed with guilt as I hurry away from the car like I'm running away from my child but I must go. Later, Mom will express concern over the possibility of carjacking with her trapped in the car and unable to leap out with the baby should some masked bandit realize that the front door is unlocked and the motor is already running. I will be annoyed by her paranoid concern but ultimately I will see her point and it will only add to my feelings of guilt.

QTY/ITEM	CAT	PRICE	TOTAL
1 Always Overnight	absorbtion	3.49	
1 Jelly beans	expansion	.69	
1 Spice drops	ditto	.59	
1 48-pack Huggies dprs	absorbtion	11.88	
		$16.65	$2,896.84

The hardware store.

QTY/ITEM	CAT	PRICE	TOTAL
1 Wastebasket, 42-qt. wh	redesign on dirty clothes/diapers	11.85	
1 Chocolate bar	support for Variety Clubs of Amer	3.00	
		$14.85	$2,911.69

The pharmacy again.

QTY/ITEM	CAT	PRICE	TOTAL
1 One-hour photo	memory enhancement	17.19	
2 York Peppermint Patties	depression	.30	
		$17.49	$2,929.18

And then there is nowhere else to go and the hands on the clock put a knot in my gut. It is almost time for another feeding. And so we drive home and go upstairs, and it's safe in the bedroom. The light is low and the smells are warm. I punch the button on the ghetto blaster that I suppose should now be called a CD player because it's playing music for a baby, and I wait for the music that will save us both.

I don't know why it works—this CD we bought called *Baby on Board* by some dame named Viva Knight—but I have chosen not to bill Callie for the disc as I believe it is, in some part, saving my sanity. Viva starts to play. The sound of a piano swells. It's quiet and sweet as it sways back and forth between Beethoven, Mozart, and Haydn and somehow finds "Twinkle, Twinkle" somewhere in the middle. It's a brilliantly simple thing, this CD. It calms Callie and it calms me. It speaks to the bittersweet confusion that lives in constant flux somewhere between my chest and my gut. Viva plays on as Callie pulls her life force out from the middle of me.

March 30 — Friday

Callie's hospital photos came today. The ridiculous ritual we muddled through just before leaving the maternity ward two weeks ago today resulted in this fabulously exciting package arriving at the house today. Callie had lain in the scoop of a scale in the hospital nursery on a big sheet of rainbowy paper that acted as background. She looked everywhere but straight up as the camera fixed above her head shot a little red laser X down on her chin and clicked away image after image. School pictures for the minute and immobile. I giggled and her father rolled his eyes as we subjected her to the stainless steel equivalent of a Sears photo shoot. Look at the bunny! Look at the respirator!

The lump in my throat was already growing as I knew the next thing we had to do involved walking out of the hospital, getting into the car, and driving away to a life and world where there were no nurses and I would be entirely responsible. I cried into Callie's little duck-covered bunting all the way home. It was a terrifying ride. So I milked our little demented photo shoot for all it was worth, knowing all the while that we were making a ridiculous sight.

But today the photos came and they are perfect and we are so, so, so glad we got them. She is beautiful and we thank God we had the good sense to order three different sizes and double copies on all of them because everyone must see them! Everyone must have one. Already they are a cherished moment that we will never see again — back when our baby was brand-new.

So, I think, that was $56.03 well spent. It was $56.03 I spent in order to ensure that Callie never questions our devotion. Like all decent parents, we are making every possible record of her existence. God forbid she should reach the age of five and be able to find one square inch of this house where some record of her does not ring out, sing out, hang, or dangle. We have photos and footprints and hospital tags. I even have a chart of her daily diaper use.

I think it's worth acknowledging that there is an entire world of expenses that are devoted solely to the future well-being of her self-esteem. There are certain purchases that must be made, expenses incurred, in order to confirm to the child that I am absolutely unconditionally and nearly (if not wholly) delusional over her perfection, beauty, and light—her simple being. These expenses may appear to be somewhat subjective and it might be thought that I shouldn't bill her for such expenses without her consent but then it would be too late. The picture would be lost to time and Callie would always wonder why we didn't value her as much on that day as the rest. Was she less a baby that day? Did she somehow disappoint? No. We cannot risk that. Everyday must be documented—every breath—at whatever cost. Callie will understand. She will be glad we did it.

QTY/ITEM	CAT	PRICE	TOTAL
1 *Oh Baby: A Journal Baby Book*	well-being/ self-esteem	$18.95	$2,948.13

April 2 — Monday

Callie and I sent a lovely basket of cookies and coffees to our doctors today. We ordered them from Dean & Deluca to ensure that our doctors know that we have style. It's a "thank you" — a thank you for splitting me open like so many barroom peanuts. Funny the things we come to appreciate.

The cost rests fairly on both of us. Some may say she deserves a say in this sort of discretionary spending but I believe it is a parenting choice. I am shaping her into a baby of fine taste and good breeding.

When she crawls down Main Street, people will tip their hats and say, "There goes a baby of distinction." At least, that's what they'd say if we all lived inside an old MGM musical, which, at this point in my babyland delusional haze, I'm not sure we don't. It seems to me I can hear tap dancers now . . . no wait, that's a baby crying.

QTY/ITEM	CAT	PRICE	TOTAL
1 Dean & Deluca biscotti/ rugelach/coffee	good breeding (50%)	$53.22	$3,001.35

April 3 — Tuesday

Her father isn't charging her for her new boom box.

I'm convinced he's doing this just to make me look bad. Forget that he has yet to be awake for a 3 A.M. feeding and I think he'd be hard-pressed to say he's had to interrupt his gym schedule since the big push, but it won't matter: In ten years she'll use this fact to hurt me.

"See! My father didn't charge me for everything he bought! You're a bad person."

Be still my tongue.

He (her father) was sent out into the world (a place I cannot visit) with an assignment—get Callie her own boom box so that we can have our radio/CD player back in the kitchen. We miss NPR.

He took the challenge and returned home with said product—a space-aged machine that will play Beethoven and "Twinkle-Twinkle," on a loop if necessary, until she is twelve.

However, when I asked for the receipt so I could add it to the tally, he looked at me incredulously, clearly indicating his shock that I might think he is the same sort of cold-blooded, money-grubbing, tough-nosed wench that I am.

"No." That's what he said.

"Whattya mean 'no'?" I asked.

"No. I took care of it."

I opened my mouth to say more but only a little exasperated, indignant "uh . . ." came out.

He has no intention of billing Callie for an expense that I believe could not more clearly be in her column. This is not an impulse or an extravagance. She *must* hear the music if she is to stop crying at midnight (or 4:30 in the afternoon) and she *must* stop crying at midnight (or 4:30 in the afternoon) because I *must* be spared my sanity as I am the one with the breasts and without those, life around here would get tough. Therefore, we *must* have a CD player and it *must* not be the one that broadcasts Garrison Keillor's *Writer's Almanac* every morning over our coffee. This is a clearly defined mandatory Callie expense. And yet, he protests—just to suck up to her.

So—thanks a lot, but you're not going to break me. Kids have to learn financial responsibility. Oprah did a whole show on it today. The tally will continue. Oprah says, "Rock on, sister!" And as for your generosity, proud papa—what can I say? You're a better man than I. You are more charitable and she will always pick you as a shopping partner as I will continue to quote Oprah until I am blue in the face and I will believe that I am right.

But there is another, sadder reality—despite how right I may feel, the tally comes with an ever-growing and unrelenting sense of guilt. I assume this nasty, gnawing feeling is just the beginning of my taking responsibility for however I am going to screw her up. It's a given—I'll mess her up. The only intrigue that remains is: How will I do it?

Will it be the tally? Am I all wrong? Or will it be those little unintentional head rolls she does when I don't catch her in just the right hold? Or perhaps it will be the sizzling spikes of rage that zap through my body when she clamps down on my tit in such a way as to make me see stars. Is it possible she can feel the rage even though I clamp down on the response the moment it begins? Could it be that my tit rage will reemerge at puberty?

I breathe through the spikes, I swear. I squelch them immediately but I have to believe she feels it. She's sucking the very life out of me, after all. How can she not know when my entire body experiences the equivalent of a high-voltage electrical jolt? Of course she knows. But maybe she doesn't care. Maybe she does.

Oh, I can see it now. In fifteen years, she will suddenly realize that tit rage has messed her up but good! It's the reason she sucks her thumb, can't pronounce her Rs, walks with a limp, and wets the bed.

She's going through a growth spurt right now, eating every ninety minutes or screaming her tiny little ass off. The truth is, she is a great baby and fusses rarely. It's just that right now she's throwin' on at least an ounce a day and that's a weighty business as it were, so she's a little high-strung at present. And, of course, so am I. In fact, I think she knows that. I think she knows that she has been born to a high-strung mother and therefore has agreed to only scream about the big shit. "I'm just gonna holler if it really counts." That's what she says to me in her contemplative moments and, of course, it makes me feel guilty — really guilty — as our vice president would say, "big time."

April 4 — Wednesday

It's early afternoon and she's already eaten five times. I ran to the car after the last feeding, promised to be back before the next one. I wanted to price out formula. I want to know exactly what she's saving.

At my local grocer, a thirteen-ounce can of prepared Similac costs $3.19. It is my understanding that an individual of Callie's size, approximately eight pounds, would consume four ounces per feeding. She is currently eating about eight times a day, which means she would consume approximately 2.46 cans of Similac a day.

Whoa! Forget the cost. I have just made the connection. She must, then, be sucking the equivalent of 2.46 of those cans out of me every day.

That's unnerving.

Bottom line, she'd be spending $7.85 a day on food. So, there you are. The sacrifice of my nipples is saving Miss Thing a bundle. That should be enough to put a little of my ever-constant whatever-the-moment-might-bring guilt to rest.

Obviously, there was no need to purchase the Similac. But I did pick up a few other items. After all, I was out.

QTY/ITEM	CAT	PRICE	TOTAL
1 Baby Clean	sanitation	2.99	
1 Jelly Beans (Black)	sanity	.69	
1 68-pack Pampers Stretch	sanitation	12.79	
		$16.47	$3,017.82

April 5 — Thursday

I called Kay, the midwife, today. Actually Lonnie called. I was too distraught with the fact that my breasts are being worked over like some kind of odds-on long shot in a prize fight. It's the growth spurt—she's eating for more than an hour, every hour. You do the math.

Kay says, "Are you trying to do anything else besides rest?"

"Yes," I say without hesitation. I have a living to make. There are contracts and writing deadlines.

"Yeah, I could hear it in your voice—the stress. That's why you're having trouble."

So this is it? It all boils down to this? I breast-feed in order to give my beloved girl all the advantages and in return, the whole of the rest of my life is cashed in?

I cannot even begin to figure out the billing on that. It boggles the mind, conjures up thoughts of millions and billions only to skid out on some existential tangent that comes crashing back down onto that equation that made the news back when I was a kid—the one that was calculated by some scientist who figured out the actual worth of the human body in elemental form. It came to somewhere in the vicinity of six dollars and thirteen cents.

What was I thinking anyway? I've been micromanaging my life for years. How did I not even consider what life would be like when I got home with this little bitty baby?

I didn't. I never once thought, "Hmm . . . I wonder what the days will be like?" No. It was more along the lines of: "Right. We'll come home from the hospital. Mom will get settled in her house. Spring will come. I'll get the garden squared away before I go back to work. Then I'll secure a new apartment in the city and then . . ."

Finally, a moment that might really have been well-served by a little micromanaging and I skimmed right over it. For those of you who have not yet bred, you should think about this: You should think about how much you value your current schedule. Already, I can tell this is not something that the unbredded among us will hear. But regardless, I will try.

This is what your baby's life will be and therefore, this is what your life will be:

5:00 A.M   Eat.
6:00 A.M.   Stop eating.
6:45 A.M.   Finally stop fussing and fall asleep.

9:30 A.M.   Wake up and eat.

10:30 A.M.   Stop eating and fuss enough to make it hard for your mother to eat.

11:30 A.M.   Stop crying and stare; let your mother check her E-mail but not for long enough to actually answer it.

11:45 A.M.   Pass out.

12:15 P.M.   Wake up, scream your ass off 'til your mom gets that you are half-starved.

12:30 P.M.   Eat.

1:30 P.M.   Stop eating and fuss until you are put into your vibrating chair.

1:45 P.M.   Fuss until you are taken out of your vibrating chair and put under your black-and-white polka-dot arches.

2:00 P.M.   Stop staring at dots and fuss until your mother realizes you are half-starved.

2:30 P.M.   Eat.

3:30 P.M.   Stop eating and fuss because you are being put into your stroller.

3:45 P.M.   Finally pass out despite a valiant fight.

4:00 P.M.   Watch *Oprah*.

4:30 P.M.   Eat while watching *Oprah*.

5:30 P.M.   Stop eating and scream all out.

6:30 P.M.   Keep screaming if at all possible.

7:00 P.M.   Enjoy early feeding thanks to relentless screaming.

8:00 P.M.   Stop eating.

8:30 P.M.   Pass out so completely that it makes your mother nervous for two reasons: (1) You

might not be breathing and (2) you'll never
sleep through the wee hours if you're so
asleep now.

11:45 P.M.   Wake up and eat.

12:45 A.M.   Stop eating and be wide awake—as wide
awake as possible.

1:45 A.M.   Smile at your mom and pass out—give her a
break and sleep until 5 A.M.

April 6 — Friday

Mom leaves Sunday. I am opting not to dwell on that fact
because I get a little queasy when I do. She's going back to
Michigan to pack up the old house and get moved out here for
good. She is leaving me for a month, leaving me with a baby
and a very sick cat.

I don't know how I will do this on my own—especially the
days when Lonnie is in the city—and of course, Monday is one
of those. Okay. I have to stop thinking about this or I will
puke. I will think about other things.

April 7 — Saturday

After careful consideration, I have decided to credit Callie with
monies not spent due to incarceration. We will categorize it under "internment rebate." I will credit her with the balance in
my wallet as I find it each Friday.

QTY/ITEM	CAT	PRICE	TOTAL
1 Credit	internment rebate	+ $74.00	($87.00)

As mentioned previously—the gifts continue to arrive on a daily basis. I feel it necessary to catalog them as they are the physical property of Miss Callie and she may, in the future, need a full accounting of her belongings should she find it necessary to pillage her estate in order to pay me back. (She could always sell her boom box, for example.)

Since birth, she has gotten: one wooden duck mobile, a Katrina doll, a Noah's ark bib, a hand-knit sweater, one yellow John Lennon–designed fleece blanket, monetary funds (deposited into her own account), a potted azalea, a "My First Catholic Bible" book set with handy carrying handle (for the record—the baby is Lutheran), one bib-flowered coverall, one yellow polka-dot coverall, one lavender jumper with shirt, a wood-cut puzzle spelling "Callie," one basket of bath and baby supplies, one extravagant cut-flower arrangement featuring tulips, a salmon-pink bean-bag pig, a black-and-white Gymini play set, two baby books, two photo albums, a pink jogging suit, one pair lambswool booties, two videos featuring black-and-white shapes, one Pat-and-Peek book, a selection of Baby Bee bath products, and one set of chopsticks in carrying case made of antique kimono silk.

April 8 — Sunday

Callie and me, we're in the back seat of the Subaru. My breasts are present and accounted for and in full view for all the gas-buying world to see. I'm changing her diaper in my lap as we sit with the motor idling alongside the Quick Mart at the Texaco station just west of Springfield, Massachusetts.

We are here because Mom headed back to Michigan today and we thought it would be a good idea to lead her up to the Mass turnpike so she wouldn't have to wind herself through the twisted backways of the Berkshires. So we did. We led her to the Mass turnpike. Our mistake is that we didn't lead her *onto* the Mass turnpike because as we waved her along — "straight on 'til morning" kind of thing — we watched in horror as she veered to the right, to the east, toward Boston, instead of to the left, to the west, toward Albany, toward Michigan.

I shouted from the backseat with my arm over Callie's chair, "Follow her!"

We did, finally catching up and passing her as she was stealing panicked looks down at her map as she drove sixty miles an hour. We gestured for her to follow us and she gave a resigned, guilty, and relieved little nod and smile.

The next exit was forty miles away in rain and fog. By the time we got there we were out of gas, the baby was hungry, she needed to be changed, and I was starved and in serious need of my one and only cup of coffee per day.

We made Mom chant, "West-Albany-West-Albany," for fifteen minutes and then we shoved her back out into the world, back onto the interstate, this time in the correct direction, and we went in search of a gas station. Lonnie headed out to search for food for me and returned muttering something about Hostess Twinkies. There was nothing but trash in the Quick Mart, he said. I was tempted to send him back for the Twinkies but even smashed into the back seat with a baby and a changing pad in my lap, I could see the enormity of my post-delivery thighs. I bit my tongue.

I looked at Lonnie with his head resting against the back of the driver's seat. I took the bird's-eye view of us—a man in the front seat, a woman in the back, a newborn, parked alongside a Texaco station, motor running, tits exposed, baby butt a mess, no food, and too much rain.

"When we ran into each other and started chatting over cocktails at that Dramatist Guild reception a few years ago, could you ever have imagined we might be here?"

"Well, if I say no," Lonnie answered without lifting his head, "it shows a lack of imagination so I hesitate to do that. But if the question is *did* I imagine this—I'd have to say no. I didn't."

By the by, Mom agrees with me; financial responsibility is well worth the pain of teaching it. She picked up some diapers yesterday and handed me the receipt for reimbursement.

QTY/ITEM	CAT	PRICE	TOTAL
1 PMP BBYFR UNS (diapers)	sanitation	$3.69	$3,021.51

I'm also considering hittin' the baby up for the water bill. The water bill, moisturizing lotion, steam damage to wall art, soap—these are the costs inherent in excessive showering, which is what I do now, what I did tonight. It's the only place where I can take a true break. I cannot hear Callie cry and therefore, I cannot feel guilt or the need to rush. So, generally I do a round of clean-up after Sophie, scrubbing down all her accidents around the house. Then, I tell Lonnie he's in charge because I'm taking my shower. I strip down, being very careful of my extremely delicate breasts. I turn on the shower, let it get good and hot, and then stand beneath the spigot and let the water beat on my face, on my back, as I think of nothing. I watch red splotches rise up on my skin. I feel the muscles in my back let down as much as they plan to. And then there is that moment when the water will bring no more relief. I must turn it off and face forward, move on. I hold my breath, give the faucet handle a fast turn, and listen for the noise. Is she crying? Is she sleeping? Is she just biding her time until she hears the water stop?

I suspect this is transitory and I will be so sad when I look around me one day and realize this moment in my life is over and I spent the entire time pining for a shower and wishing it would end.

After my shower tonight, I sat in the armchair holding her and crying, her loudly, me silently. "I'm not cut out for this," I whispered as I laid her across my lap and moved my legs back and forth, keeping the rhythm constant, moving her toward peace and quiet.

"I'm not good at it and I don't like it," I choked out.

Lonnie petted my head, my shower-wet hair.

"I love her but I don't like this."

"I know," he said.

I'm so afraid that I will not come to the point of joy that Callie deserves. She is an exemplary baby and she deserves to be appreciated as such. She deserves to live amidst joy—not amidst showers and sobbing.

April 9—Monday

The sun finally shines.
The stroller finally rolls.
It is sixty degrees.
We are allowed out into the world.
Goodness prevails.
I can handle this.

QTY/ITEM	CAT	PRICE	TOTAL
2 Pediatrician visits co-pay	baby maintenance	$30.00	$3,051.51

April 12—Thursday

Tomorrow is Good Friday and Friday the thirteenth. Today is Maundy Thursday—whatever that is. I called the vet today. Sophie will be put to sleep on Saturday.

April 13—Friday

QTY/ITEM	CAT	PRICE	TOTAL
1 Credit	internment rebate	+ $130.00	($217.00)

April 14 — Saturday

She's gone.

Subj: Sophie Small and Orange
Date: 4/14

Because I thought you might like to know and because I need to tell you:
  Sophie the cat died today.
  She was here at home on her big chair. She went into a very deep sleep and from there she passed on. The baby cried as Sophie was given a sedative and then, as if Sophie was breezing through her, Callie, too, fell asleep and slept peacefully for about an hour. I suspect that Sophie breezed through all of us but Callie is the one who was wise enough to feel it. I can only hope that as she passed through she left a bit of her gumption and spirit with my little baby girl. That would be a true gift.
  Once upon a time, I wrote this about Sophie:
  "It is Sophie who holds the secret: to be lost in love, to dance and sing with joy, to live where there are no doubts, no questions of identity, who she is or how it happened. To be orange and small and to never want for tiger stripes or thumbs."
  That was my little cat and I miss her.
  Betsy

And the baby smiled today. She smiled at her dad.

April 16 — Monday

QTY/ITEM	CAT	PRICE	TOTAL
1 PMP BBYFR ORIG (diapers)	sanitation	$5.99	$3,057.50

April 17 — Tuesday

I have spent an inordinant amount of time sticking the pacifier in Callie's mouth today. I've had to — I've had to sleep. I'm so tired. I think it's the combination of a tiny baby, a dead cat, and a spring that refuses to get its ass in gear. I'm a bit spent and I really have had enough of this never-ending tear festival. The new-baby hormone downpour was enough — I didn't need the dead cat torrent, too.

It occurred to me earlier today, as I sneezed while sitting on the couch nursing my child and immediately had to consider what protection I was wearing on my lower half, that this child has left me leaking on both ends and in the middle. I can't stop crying and I can't stop peeing, my tits leak, and I can't tell you how many kegels I do every damn day.

I'm sounding cranky. I acknowledge that. But here's the upside: all this has made me realize why counting receipts and totaling tallies is a worthwhile endeavor. It's answerable. It's graspable. There is a right and a wrong. I cannot explain why my baby cries. I don't know why my cat had to suffer so much. I do not know how long it will take for the men in D.C. to realize that cold weather in spring and summer *is*, in fact, global warming. But I can add $1.79 to $15.22 to $4.83 and I can do it all day and it's never going to baffle me. It will always be a task I can accomplish because I can add.

To that end, I've had a few more expenses. I'll admit I was a little slow on the uptake but it occurred to me recently that just because the baby has me captive here in this house doesn't mean I can't get on-line. She hasn't cut the phone lines—yet.

So, from MotherhoodNursing.com, I've added a few items to my wardrobe. Trust me, these shirts are butt ugly and the best I could do—I would *never* purchase *or* wear any of them if I wasn't delivering milk every 90 to 120 minutes. The kid is definitely paying up on this one.

QTY/ITEM	CAT	PRICE	TOTAL
1 Ditsy floral turtleneck— single center nursing slit	easy access wardrobe	6.99	
1 Short sleeve chambray blue shirt—horizontal flap w/ double nursing slits	lunch-friendly wardrobe	29.00	
1 Short sleeve crew neck tee—single center nursing slit	lacto-centric wardrobe	19.00	
1 Comfortable supportive sports bra for nursing moms	flap-happy wardrobe	15.00	
		69.99	
Tax and Shipping		11.45	
		$81.44	$3,138.94

April 18 — Wednesday

I have freaked myself out completely.

I have bought and paid for an airline ticket that will allow Callie and me to travel to Grand Rapids, Michigan, (by way of Detroit) on May 1. We will be on our own, just Callie and me.

Oh, God.

It's a mistake. Call me spineless and shallow, but I do care what people think and I really don't want to be that person I have despised for twenty years. You know the one I mean. She sits up front, gets the most leg room, and has a baby that cries *the entire time you're on the plane!*

Oh, God.

But I have to go back. It'll be the last time I'm in Mom's house. I have to help her pack. And Dad needs some real time with Callie now that we've recovered from that nasty delivery business. He needs to know I will continue to come "home" even when Mom lives out here. We will not disappear. We are still family. I'll be glad to be there, I'm sure. But—getting there . . .

Oh, God.

First things first: I had to order a portable crib/bassinet/playpen thingee. This is a must-have item according to more than a few friends. Callie will use it whenever we go away for a night and it can be her crib at Mom's house. Clearly, it's a necessary expense. She can't exactly throw down her sleeping bag on a cot, can she?

So, from babiesrus.com:

QTY/ITEM	CAT	PRICE	TOTAL
1 Pack n Play w/ bassinet/ parent organizer	portability	99.99	
1 Pack n Play sheet— bordeaux gingham	decor	9.99	
		109.98	
Tax and Shipping		14.85	
		$124.83	$3,263.77

I did not get her a separate ticket as my doctor suggested she would probably feel more secure in my lap. And, according to many friends and the doctor, I will need to breast-feed her during takeoff and landing to keep her ears from clogging.

I need to think about something else for a while.

April 19 — Thursday

The nursing shirts arrived today. As pictured, they are butt ugly. But they are slitted, double-slitted, single-slitted, center/side/horizontal slitted and therefore, worth their price. I'm tired of finding myself at the post office with my shirt unbuttoned. It's time we address some of these resocialization issues. I'm going to be back out in the world eventually and it would be best if I were fully dressed.

As my beloved OB-GYN said the morning after the big push, "Breast-feeding is perfectly natural but it's not naturally perfect." This is the same doctor who likened labor to driving up to the Berkshires from the city. "You can spend days on the West Side Highway just trying to get out of town but that doesn't mean that once you hit six eighty-four you won't get here in a flash."

Anyway, nothin' for nothin', but do you know how one determines whether breast-feeding is going well? That is to say, that the babe is getting sufficient milk, enough nutrition, adequate bulk?

You count diapers. Every day. Every diaper. Separate the wet from the dirty and tally the total.

It makes sense, I guess. Since you can't tell what's going in, you gotta count what's comin' out. And by the by, what comes out looks like a Jackson Pollack exhibit. Of course, they didn't tell me that—they told me everything else but not that—and that's why I ended up in the doctor's office on the Monday morning after she was born having only just left the hospital two days before. By Sunday night, Pollack paint was absolutely pouring out of her and the doctor on call just kept saying, "It's probably not even diarrhea," which meant absolutely nothing to me because what else could it be? So finally she instructed us to bag the diaper and come in to the office on Monday. So I did. I bagged the very next diaper. And then I bagged each diaper after that just so that the medical team would have absolutely everything they might need to diagnose her.

When I arrived at the office, I got completely freaked out at how many sick kids there were in the waiting room. I mean, come on! It's a pediatrician's office. Why do they allow all these sick kids to be here? My daughter could get infected. They're coughing and spewing their nasty, snot-nosed germs on my tiny goddess! I stayed hunkered over her carrier, defending her against invaders until the nurse called us in. When the doctor entered the room, I handed him the bag. By then, it was filled with five Ziploc bags each containing an original Pollack. The doctor took a glance at the Ziplocs and said, "Yup, that's a breast-fed baby's diaper."

So why didn't anyone tell me?

I need to find someone new to bill because that fifteen-dollar co-pay really shouldn't be Callie's or my responsibility.

Anyway, I have a chart now that tracks her diaper count, wet and dirty, and her feedings. Mom says that when she gets older I will have to change the "dirty" to something else because we don't want her to think anything her body does is dirty. Okay. I have two things to say to that: 1. If she's capable of reading her own chart *and yet* she's still tossing off diapers, our troubles go deeper than what's dirty and what's not; and 2. that's the most ridiculous pile of woo-woo, politically correct, horse kaka I have ever heard.

Of course our bodies make stuff that's dirty. What do you think they spent the Middle Ages trying to figure out as they waded through the dead bodies and hacking masses? Why have we spent thousands of years evolving to the point of indoor plumbing if not to finally understand that our waste (repeat *waste*) is dirty? This reasoning is right up there with the brain-dead parental masses who righteously claim their children should not be immunized because, because, oh who cares why! These folks need to spend an afternoon in an old cemetery where they can mosey through the tombstones and read the names of five, six, seven children—all with the same last name—who died within ten days of each other. Nothing like a good plague to bring you back down to earth, as it were, if I may.

I do not intend to change the wording. The diapers will be considered dirty if they are.

The more important question is this: Do I save these charts as part of Calllie's baby book? Will she want to see how many diapers she went through at two weeks, four weeks? Will she care that I took great pride in the fact that, on many days, she had as many as seven dirty diapers? I mean, that's impressive. But that's my baby. She's ambitious. You say, "Give me dirty diapers," and she says, "How high?"

If you are wondering whether these diapers are disposable or cloth—I will tell you. They are, to date, disposable. I still intend to go for the cloth but the first time I tried to put one on her, she got lost in one of the folds. That is to say, she's just too small for the diapers I got.

I feel wholly unsupported in this effort. Where are the militant Green women with their clotheslines and burlap-bag dresses? Where are the women who will tell me I can do this? Where is Ralph Nader? Strike that. I don't want to talk to Ralph Nader. I'm still bitter.

All I'm saying is, in another time, I would have been sold the correct diapers.

Maybe I've got it all wrong anyway. My neighbor says it's pretty much a wash (no pun intended) as to which is worse for the environment since cloth diapers take loads of energy and resources to keep clean. However, I wonder if that equation includes the energy needed to manufacture the disposables and not just the disposing of the disposables. After all, it must take loads of energy and resources to create such a convenient little absorbent item. But of course, something must get spent spinning that cotton into diapers, too. Oy.

At present, Callie is going through approximately one 68-pack of diapers a week and creating one tall-sized garbage bag full of refuse a week. However, personally, I believe she could cut back. There are times when she is clearly just amusing her-self by going through as many diapers as possible before I ac-tually get one all the way on. She lays there acting innocent, kicking and cooing, and then just as I'm taping a clean one shut—Jackson Pollack. I told her she's only ruining the planet for herself. I'll be dead and gone and she'll be left to deal with the dire results of her diaper binging as she tries to raise her children on a mountain of garbage in a world with no trees.

Yes. I realize that might be a harsh thing to say to a new-born but I have to tell you, she barely seemed to care.

Anyway, I am going to use the cloth. I am. But let's face it, it's not like I don't have a few years to figure this out.

In the meantime:

QTY/ITEM	CAT	PRICE	TOTAL
1 68-pack Pampers Stretch	sanitation	$12.79	$3,276.56

April 20 — Friday

My friend Amie E-mailed me today about coming to visit soon. She said, "I can't wait to see Callie and the mother in you." The mother in me? Well, for starters—she's a big woman. Far big-ger than anything I ever imagined, and this is coming from a woman who has never been considered petite.

I have my six-week checkup next week. I have made a vow that I will begin the serious dig-out from this fat after that weigh-in. And I'll tell you right here and right now, I am not looking forward to that moment. I don't want to see the num-ber. It's gonna smart.

And of course, my agent called with an audition this week. I hemmed and hawed my way out of it and suggested I might not be ready for another month or so. I won't be in shape by then either but perhaps it won't be quite so horrifying. God forbid, my agent or any casting director sees me in my present state. That would be the end. I would be burned in their memory file forever as the mammoth mama. I would never get another audition again.

And that, I'm afraid, would cost Miss Callie a small fortune.

Presently, however, we are not dealing with that possibility and in fact, she has earned herself another rebate.

QTY/ITEM	CAT	PRICE	TOTAL
1 Credit	internment rebate	+ $115.00	($332.00)

April 21 — Saturday

QTY/ITEM	CAT	PRICE	TOTAL
1 Vitamins	milk insurance	15.99	
1 Board book Black & White	mental stimulation	4.95	
1 Plush book Spots & Stripes	mental stimulation	8.99	
		$29.93	$3,306.49

April 23 — Monday

What if I forget I have a baby? This is a reoccurring thought.

What if tomorrow, say, I just get up from the other side of the bed so that I don't see her and I get dressed and head to the diner for some breakfast? There are moments when, after she has been asleep for a good long while, I find I am suddenly startled and unnerved by the thought that there is a child upstairs that I have not thought about for two, maybe three, minutes.

In these moments it occurs to me that I could possibly forget that I have a child altogether and as a result neglect her in some irreparable way. It wouldn't be intentional. I would simply forget to remember. I've lived several decades without a child. I have had one now for not even six weeks. I think it's possible that it could just slip my mind and I could leave her somewhere, or forget to take her somewhere, or worst of all, look at her and wonder where her mother is.

This is, perhaps, as good a reason as any to continue to acquire things. The more reminders there are around me that there is a baby in the house, the more likely I am to remember.

From Staples:

QTY/ITEM	CAT	PRICE	TOTAL
3 Mesh baskets, large	wardrobe de-chaos	$22.47	$3,328.96

From the pharmacy:

QTY/ITEM	CAT	PRICE	TOTAL
1 68-pack Pampers Stretch	same old same old	12.79	
1 Evenflo nurse pads	personal dignity	6.29	
		$19.08	$3,348.04

April 25 — Wednesday

My baby has a cold. It's her very first. I've spent the last twenty-four hours staring up her nose, particularly her right nostril. Finally, this morning, after hearing the whistle of hidden snot for most of the day before, I actually witnessed a little bit of baby snot moving back and forth in her tiny little nostril as she breathed. I immediately called Dr. Brown.

We snagged a 3:15 P.M. appointment. Of course, by then there was no more baby snot. However, there was enough baby-snot residue that I didn't look like a total hysterical, reactionary doofus. It has been officially declared that she, in fact, does have a cold. Dr. Brown looked deep into her ears and nose, listened to her chest. The only symptom he could find was the stuffy nose, but that was enough.

She's been so sweet about it, I feel bad billing her. She's barely even fussing, though I can hear her whistling as she breathes. She's upstairs right now, asleep in her bassinet with her new vaporizer moisturizing the air.

As I said, I hate to kick her when she's down but colds are not for free.

QTY/ITEM	CAT	PRICE	TOTAL
1 Doctor's visit	co-pay on baby maintenance	15.00	
1 Ayr Saline Mist	natal nasal clarity	3.99	
1 Kaz humidifier	air quality control	27.99	
1 Pediacare drops	drugs	5.59	
1 Farley spice drops	mother's care & feeding	.88	
		$53.45	$3,401.49

April 26 — Thursday

Well, there you have it. My six-week checkup has come and gone.

Much like my figure.

I have forty pounds to lose.

Okay. Forty-three.

The numbers on a scale go up so much higher than I ever realized.

Oh.

Lord.

Pass the spice drops.

April 28 — Saturday

QTY/ITEM	CAT	PRICE	TOTAL
1 Credit	internment rebate	+ $50.00	($382.00)

April 30 — Monday

Tomorrow I get on a plane with a snot-filled, seven-week-old, adorable, but oh-so-slightly cranky baby. Why should that create such anxiety? I am hobbled with anxiety. It keeps me up at 3 A.M. when she's sleeping soundly.

Is it really about a bunch of dirty looks from people I'll never see again? What's the worst thing that could happen? She could cry at the airport in Hartford. She could cry from Hartford to Detroit. She could cry in Detroit. She could cry from Detroit to Grand Rapids. She could spit up and do that choking thing that thoroughly freaks me out. She could go beyond crying into that screeching thing that makes the human ear ring and sends dogs burrowing under couches. We could be delayed on the tarmac for fourteen hours.

That last one probably won't happen.

But it could.

Sometimes I find talking these things out with a few select friends can help alleviate anxiety.

Alice says, "It'll probably be fine but if it's not and she cries the whole way, then it's an excruciating few hours but then it's over."

My neighbor Mary says, "Don't be anxious. If you are, she'll be."

Erica says "Breast-feed on takeoff and landing."

Jackie agrees but says, "*Don't* wake her up if she's asleep."

Susan says, "Bring a rattle and her favorite blanket."

Marisa says, "Carry as little as possible."

Karen says, "Actually, it's kind of great. It's the one time that stewardesses are nice to you. You might consider always carrying a baby along."

Tory says, "Have that tit ready."

My stepmother says, "I hear they have these new baby earplugs that work miracles with the pressure change."

Lonnie says, "Just breathe."

My mom says, "Are you sure you want to do this, honey?"

My friend Laura sent a package of three new outfits. The note said, "I figured she needed something new for her trip. If she's going to scream and drive everyone crazy, at least she'll look cute."

I'm considering billing Callie for the ticket after all. But I know that's just spite talking. It's defendable however. All this chaos, all this change, this unearthing of entrenched patterns and routines. It's all on her. She may only be nine pounds and change at this point, but she knows how to throw that weight around.

She's turned my true-blue Midwestern mom into a New Englander and Dad into putty—a state in which he remains with all babies until they begin to speak and voice their opinions. She's turned my methadoned, street-bound brother into an uncle (which might just be his first title with a positive twist), and Randy into an executor. She's made my seventeen-year-old half sister wholly an aunt and my stepmother of twenty-plus years something more but we can't figure out what to call it. And then there's me and I cannot be the judge except to say, it would be a shorter list to name the things that are not changed.

She seems to have the power to change everything but her diaper. To which I say, baby, change thyself. And change planes while you're at it.

Here is the plan for tomorrow:

8:00 A.M.	Wake up
	Breast-feed
9:45 A.M.	Breast-feed
10:00 A.M.	Depart house
11:00 A.M.	Arrive at airport
	Diaper change
12:05 A.M.	DEPART HARTFORD
	while breast-feeding
1:50 P.M.	Breast-feed
1:59 P.M.	ARRIVE DETROIT
	while breast-feeding
	Diaper change
3:15 P.M.	DEPART DETROIT
	while breast-feeding
3:55 P.M.	Breast-feed
4:03 P.M.	ARRIVE GRAND RAPIDS
	while breast-feeding

Packing List

CALLIE:
～

3 sleepers
2 short rompers
3 pairs socks
1 hat
1 spare outfit in
  diaper bag
3 blankets
1 bottle baby soap
2 towels
2 washcloths
diapers
Desitin
2 cloth diapers
nasal syringe
Get Smart video
black/white pattern
  picture (Callie art)
3 rattles
2 pacifiers
3 books
Gimini Playset
vibrating chair (?)
watch
car seat
stroller frame
diaper chart

ME:
～

toothbrush
underwear
camera
Lansinoh nipple
  ointment
cell phone

May 1 — Tuesday

I hadn't put two and two together until now, somewhere over Cleveland, sitting next to the happiest baby on the planet. She is hanging out in her own (free) seat making faces and smiling like a lunatic. I even got a third free seat on my left side when I pulled out baby's lunch at takeoff. Suddenly, my neighbor decided there might be a free seat further forward in the cabin.

I realized this morning that today is May 1—as in May Day, as in Mayday! Mayday! S.O.S.! With a seven-week-old baby, I'm getting on a plane full of bad air and mean grownups with nasty glares. Mayday!

But perhaps I worried needlessly. I suppose that's possible. Everything is fine. She's a dream. So far.

And it's sort of nice to be on a plane again. Something in it feels like a reentry into my life. Generally, I have been a traveling kind of person, going all over and going often. But pregnancy and puking put a crimp in that style. I have not been on a plane since before I found myself in the family way. It's hard to believe but it's been an entire year since I have left earth.

May 4 — Friday

I am in the bathroom constructing a medium-size box. We are three days into one of the more exhausting weeks of recent time. May I just say here and now, packing up the contents of your mother's house while caring for a fairly new human being is not a good idea. Simply put, it's an excellent example of bad management. However, there's no going back now. We've got very little time left and so many rooms to pack.

I am about to begin packing up the contents of the bathroom cupboard as Callie is taking one of her fifteen-minute naps, which is all she seems to take during the day anymore.

I hear Mom from her bedroom. She says, "Oh my," and her voice has a strange tint to it.

I look in on her. She is packing up her dresser. "What?" I ask.

She holds up a pill bottle. "My suicide stash," she says calmly.

I walk over to her and take the bottle. There are twenty-five or thirty pills inside. The label is dated 1979, the year Dad left. She had stockpiled sleeping pills, enough to kill herself.

"Gonna throw them out?" I ask.

"I guess I don't need them anymore." She tosses the bottle into the trash. "Guess I never did."

I remember what my friend Sharon said when I drove her by Mom's new house. Sharon is, among many other things, a serious numerologist. When she saw the address on Mom's house she said, "Hmm. Forty-three. That represents overcoming hopelessness after a breakdown."

I know Mom loves her house here in Michigan, but personally I'm glad she's leaving it. To me, it will always be the place where she crash-landed after the explosion, where she wandered aimlessly in the dark and sobbed into our dog's fur. It's where she licked her wounds and then found it in herself to get back to standing.

Hopelessness after a breakdown? It's been twenty years. I wonder if there's a statute of limitations on that "overcoming" business, numerologically speaking. I'm going to guess not since I'm beginning to suspect that the whole point of this life we get is to recover from this life we get.

May 5—Saturday

The baby simply refuses to help. Mom and I have been busting our humps all week to get this damn house packed up and she just lays there, won't pack a thing. Therefore, it has become necessary to stop packing and drive to USA Baby to purchase a Baby Bjorn Baby Carrier, even though we have a Snugli carrier at home that was a fine gift given to us by my friend Susan and her daughter, Bing.

But never mind that, Callie lies about and grouses that she's not being tended to. Therefore, if the glasses are going to get wrapped and the linens packed, the girl will have to shoulder the burden of the Bjorn Borg purchase. I need two hands.

QTY/ITEM	CAT	PRICE	TOTAL
1 Baby Bjorn Carrier— Nvy Tr	hands	$79.99	$3,481.48

And while we're on the subject, thank God Mom's neighbor has a brand-new grandchild and a collection of her own baby stuff. Thanks to young Chloe, the neighbor grandchild, we have procured a vibrating chair that I had hoped to bring from home but simply couldn't fit in the luggage.

A vibrating chair is essential. I suspect it is a registered narcotic. The effect is very much like that of checking into a low-rent, thin-sheeted, sleaze-bag motel, throwing a quarter in the box, and laying there mindlessly and anonymously vibrating away until your time runs out. Callie digs it on a cellular level. I suspect the baby has a strong inner-tramp, just digs the feeling of a cheap motel. Whatever. It buys me minutes at a time, in five-minute chunks. Time where I have both my hands.

Obviously, we could not return the vibrating chair to Chloe's grandmother without some kind of gift of appreciation. While at USA Baby, Callie chose a fetching black-white-and-red wrist rattle, a token of her appreciation for all the cheap thrills.

QTY/ITEM	CAT	PRICE	TOTAL
1 Wrist rattle—bright	business gift	$3.99	$3,485.47

May 6 — Sunday

At six o'clock tonight, as we were taping up box number seventy-two (with twenty-three more yet to pack), I looked at Mom. "So," I asked, "are you completely freaked out or do you feel like we're getting it under control?"

"I'm completely freaked out," she replied. "I'm assuming you wanted a real answer."

There was a little smile in her voice but not enough to put one on her face that, by the way, was drawn tight as a drum. Her hunched back nearly moans by itself it's in so much pain. I have to wonder just what is the real price of all of this. I'm beginning to feel like I'm ripping her out of the wallpaper of this house and she's leaving behind wide swaths of her skin.

May 7—Monday

Mom's house is empty. It's no longer Mom's house, even though she's still there, now scouring sinks and sweeping the bare, open, spacious floors. The house echoes. Her belongings, all 9,000-plus pounds of them, are on a truck headed for Connecticut by way of Cleveland and perhaps Maine.

I am lying on the bed in my oldest brother's old room at my father's house, which once was our family's house. Callie is gurgling and cooing next to me in her spiffy Pack N Play bassinet and play yard. She's reading the assembly directions that are printed in black on a white panel that's sewn to the bed. You might think she is just mesmerized because of the black and white, her two favorite colors, but that's clearly not true because she is reading aloud, albeit in a language I don't speak.

Oh. She just got to the part about the fifteen-pound weight limit. She sounds alarmed. I think.

We're very tired. It's hard to pack up your mother's life, not to mention expensive. Mom has shelled out a pretty penny, but Callie was good enough to pick up the tip for the movers. She even sprang for their noon-time pizza. Seems appropriate as Mom is starting to buckle beneath the ever-growing number under "Move" on her budget. It's into the serious thousands and as we've discussed many times, none of this would be happening without our girl.

QTY/ITEM	CAT	PRICE	TOTAL
2 14" pizzas	generosity	25.00	
2 Sodas—liter bottle	courtesy	4.16	
1 Tip to movers	bribery	140.00	
		$169.16	$3,654.63

May 8 — Tuesday

This has been some kind of no fun. It's 8:30 in the A.M. I am
once again alone with Callie in my father's house. Everyone
left for work more than an hour ago and, of course, Dad left
days ago to catch fish in Belize.

I'm waiting for Mom. She'll be here soon to pick up Callie's
Pack N Play. She's driving it back to Connecticut along with
the rest of her belongings that did not go on the truck yesterday, including Mao the cat. She will leave this morning.

Cindy will pick Callie and me up at 10:30 to take us to the
airport, where I will face my last bastion of fear — the return trip.

It's a lot of logistics. One long juggle that will culminate on
Friday when the truck arrives in my little New England town
and leaves all my mom's stuff behind, effectively transforming
my little town into our little town. And thusly, our new life will
begin. Mom and I will live down the street from each other
after more than twenty years of living on opposite sides of a
time zone.

I am eight weeks removed from the big push. My body is
healed. My support team is in place. I will return to work in a

month. Here it starts, the real deal. Now we begin to know exactly what life will look like, what's new, what's changed, what's left, and what's gone for good.

May 9 — Wednesday

Yesterday, when Cindy dropped us off at the Gerald R. Ford International Airport, it was awkward saying good-bye. We both understood that this was the official end of an era that stretches back to our adolescence. It was the last time I would be home at Mom's house, the last time she and Diane would stop by to hang like we were fifteen. When I come back now it will be something else—like grown-ups, like parents.

Say what you will about hanging your hat and where your heart is—there's a fair part of home that can only ever be that place you were when you were a kid.

May 10 — Thursday

Lonnie, as instructed, purchased child-safety latches as we will soon (although I can't imagine it from here) have a crawling, reaching baby on our hands and will need to secure the poisons. For some reason that I cannot understand because I am female and he is male, he only purchased two sets of latches and so that is the sum total of what I will bill at present.

He said he only got two because he thought we could test them out first before we invested in a full compliment. I don't understand what that means. The cupboards have to be latched and these are the child-safety latches. What's to test?

QTY/ITEM	CAT	PRICE	TOTAL
2 Child safety latch	lock down	$3.37	$3,658.00

By the by and not for nothin', I now have thirty-seven pounds to lose.

May 12 — Saturday

Lonnie's left for Chicago for five days. I must remember to tell him he can't do that anymore. He can't just leave me like this. Mom is down the street but he is still the dad and he needs to be here.

Plus, when he leaves, it makes me the grown-up, the one in charge completely. I mean, that's what I am anyway but he has no right to drive the point home.

May 13 — Sunday

The truck delivered all of Mom's things to 43 Railroad Street today. Callie coughed up the balance of the tip to the movers, ensuring a safe and happy end to the trek of the really expensive and fragile antique furniture.

QTY/ITEM	CAT	PRICE	TOTAL
1 Tip to movers	expensive appreciation	$140.00	$3,798.00

May 14—Monday

My first Mother's Day.

I was given a lovely multicolored summer clutch. It was from Callie and the cats, Vinny, Olga, and Jackie. The card had a little orange cat on the front. It was all very nice except Lonnie was in Chicago and Callie spent the whole day wailing. Mom is unpacking her house and knee-deep in "Where in the hell am I gonna put this?" So, I carried around the girl for the better part of the day, with that constant bounce in my step that could wear down a triathlete. If I put her down, she would scream. The rules were clear.

I've never witnessed Callie cry as hard as she did last night. I couldn't even get her changed and dressed because she'd scream so hard she'd start to choke herself and that, of course, completely freaked me out. I finally gave up and left her in a T-shirt that was half on half off. I called Mom in panicked tears and told her she had to come over. I was swearing and shouting to be heard over my baby's wails. At eight o'clock, I started to nurse Callie and just didn't stop until she was milked-out and nodding like a junkie. Mom took her so that I could take a shower and finally, by eleven, she passed out for four hours.

I'll be honest. It didn't cost me a cent. I can't bill her for anything, but days like that—they come at a price and even now, the next day, I'm spent.

May 16 — Wednesday

I received the numbers for Callie's bank account today. She now has an actual savings with, I might add, a handsome balance (for a two-month-old) thanks to her grandpa, grandma E., and good pal Rhonda. If she cared to, she could begin paying off her debt immediately, though I'm not pushing for her to do so as that would be gauche and untoward.

I don't know why but I get such a kick out of seeing Callie's name on official documents like bank statements and social security cards. In some sense, these are the things that drag you down in life, the nuts and bolts of the workaday world. But they are also the things that make you of this world, for the good and the bad. They are the necessities of working and living that are the necessities of existing and being.

There is evidence in every direction that I am right to be doing this — this tally business. To understand the value of time vs. material objects vs. money vs. work vs. play and so on — it's priceless. This tally will be a very good thing for Callie. I don't care how many times I have to tell her.

The Middle of the Night

Dear Callie,

Always beware letters that have been written in the middle of the night. They are bound to be filled with a certain kind of reason and clarity — or lack thereof. Read them as such.

I'm so sorry, baby girl. I know I have been short with you in the last few days. I have not handled your crying in a way of which I can be proud. I'm just praying I haven't screwed you up too completely yet. You're such a good baby. You deserve a stressless mama. I am feeling very much on my own these days and you are getting the short stick on that deal. With a father and a gramma all within arm's reach, we are the last two folks on earth that should be alone. But Gramma's still trying to get settled and your father has gone missing.

He returned home from Chicago last night and I immediately told him that we had to come up with a new plan between us, a more equal sharing of time with you. He said he completely "gets it," totally understands, and will give me no argument. Then he outlined his schedule for the next several days and, of course, he can't be here. He reminded me that he had told me of all these important lunches and meetings several weeks ago.

To that, I wanted to say to him (but didn't because of my personal vow to never have a fight in front of you): *I'm in babyland! Do you honestly think that telling me two weeks in advance that you are going to a luncheon and that you have a meeting will register as back-to-back events that are coming on the tail of five days in Chicago?! Have you ever been in babyland? There are no calendars and you are not legally allowed to look more than three minutes into the future. There is no self and anything that smacks of the outside world doesn't register without incessant repetition.*

But of course, he has not been in babyland. And that is the whole point.

I'm sorry again, baby girl. It is not for you to hear all of this but since we are in that no-man's land of the middle of the night and this is a letter you will not read because you are sixty-three days old and do not know how to read, I will continue.

I talked it out with an old friend recently. I said that I wish he would take some initiative in this new world of domesticity. Initiative? The friend smiled, said, "He's not going to take initiative with anything that has to do with anyone but himself. But, he's very good at doing what he's told. Just tell him what to do. Say, 'The grass is getting long. It's needs to be cut. You should cut the grass.' And then he'll do it."

I asked the friend, "Is that Lonnie or is that just men?"

"It's men," the friend said. "That's the way they are. Their brains don't work the same way women's do."

I remember something I saw on *Oprah* a long time ago. As we all know by now, the right and left sides of the brain handle very different kinds of jobs. One handles emotions and one handles logistics. In order to be fully functioning, however, information must travel back and forth between the two lobes. According to the *Oprah* show, studies have indicated that in women, the connective tissue between the two lobes is substantial. It's like an eight-lane superhighway with high-speed bullet trains running alongside. Information passes exceedingly quickly.

Men, on the other hand, or the other lobe as it were, have what amounts to an old path running through a cornfield that is hard to see in the off-season and impossible to see with the corn at full height, which it always is in a man's mind. In order to get information back and forth, you need to schedule an emergency airlift.

This explains, for me, why the woman almost always is the one to say "I love you" first. She can run the emotion back and forth through both lobes and come up with the conclusion that she has fallen in love. Often times, when given this information, the man stares dumbly. This is because he is nowhere near reaching that same conclusion despite the fact that he is experiencing all the same emotions.

Six months later, after a woman is long gone from frustration and hurt, the information will have finally reached the other lobe. Our man will bang the side of his head much like "I coulda had a V-8" and say, "Damn! I love her, too!"

This also explains something about multitasking women and single-focused men. It's not that your father is self-centered, it's just that he is unable to handle more than one thought at a time. He starts with himself and he is such a big subject that he never gets to the next one.

So, since we know that the connective-tissue issue will never allow men to be multitaskers, we must take another approach. We must get your father to start with you and get to himself second. Because, as we know, baby girl, you are the very biggest subject there is. There's no getting over you.

May 18 — Friday

QTY/ITEM	CAT	PRICE	TOTAL
1 Credit	internment rebate	+ $118	($500.00)

May 21 — Monday

I just received a phone call from my old friend Jesse. He is offering up his crib for Callie to use since he is done using it.
Well, not him, really. He's been in a big bed for as long as I've
known him. No. This crib is actually the property of young
Sophia, daughter of Jesse and Gabrielle. Three-year-old Sophia
has graduated to a big bed and therefore, her parents are desperately trying to clear just the smallest of spaces for themselves in a lovely house that has become more and more
Sophia's and less and less theirs over the last three years.

This is a whole other issue, the value of space — especially
when you're the one who's paying for it and the kid is the one
who's taking it over.

As my father said on the night my water broke, "Say good-
bye to your house. It will never look this good again." (You
must read comments by my father with a small smile on your
lips. Otherwise, you might conclude he's a bit negative, which
should not be assumed.)

The crib is just one part of an unbelievable and constant

flow of freebies. Packages for Callie arrive nearly daily. She cries if we leave the post office without something large and addressed to her. I am going to have to deal with this behavior eventually. She must come to understand that for much of her life she will need to learn to get through days at a time without a gift. Sometimes entire weeks might go by without a present.

Callie's free crib is in natural wood, unlike the crib we were considering, which was a lovely white that would match her changing table. However, the white crib is priced at four hundred dollars. The natural wood crib will cost zero dollars. Since zero dollars is less than four hundred dollars, we're opting for zero dollars in natural wood.

While we're on the subject, I think it's time for another accounting of recent receipts; that is, the things Callie has recently received, not the receipts of things she has recently bought, although I will get to them in a moment because it occurs to me that I have gotten lax on the thank-you note front. Not that I haven't been sending them, because I have, but I have not billed for a good long while, not a red cent for any of it. There is the postage and the stationery and envelopes to consider and the numbers are mounting. Sure, I've been printing out digitially created cards onto white paper obtained in ways I don't care to acknowledge. So I will only bill Callie for the cost of one color print cartridge. I'll even comp the envelopes since they're just old ones I had laying around and that's the kind of generous soul I am.

QTY/ITEM	CAT	PRICE	TOTAL
18 Stamps @.34 per	office supplies/ etiquette	6.12	
1 Brother print cartridge	office supplies/ manners	42.99	
		$49.11	$3,847.11

It is important that you pay attention to these gifts and hand-me-downs. They play an important role. My goal with this journal/spreadsheet (in addition to getting my money back) has been from the beginning to perform a kind of social service, a true accounting of a baby's first year. I want people to know what they're about to face. I want them to have a firm grasp on a hard number before they roll around and make themselves one of these little bundles of sweetness and light. So listen up. You can't assume you'll be getting these give-aways. That would be bad form. And so, you must budget for all the possible expenses.

Speaking of free lunches, since last accounting Callie has received: a pewter frame; one silver spoon with a rabbit head; one silver spoon with a pink bow; a rocking horse candle; a Tibetan deity picture frame; a Cuban playsuit; a rubber snake; three jumpers; two summer outfits; a hand-painted personalized child-size chair; a stuffed cat with baby cat; a zebra hat; a black-and-white book; one "Princess" Beanie Baby doll; two shorts outfits; one violet dress, hat, and sock ensemble; a handmade quilt; a cow onesie; three wraparounds; two plastic rolling toys; teething tablets; a Baby Gap gift certificate; a cat-headed towel; three short-sleeved onesies; one yellow hat; a board book; one sleeper, and a bunny rabbit rattle.

As for the hand-me-downs, they have included a snowsuit, several outdoor fleece ensembles, and countless 12-month outfits that will be perfect for next spring. I have two sources for this endless march of lightly used clothing: Tory and two-year-old Lucie and Susan and eighteen-month-old Bing.

Tory and Susan ship these things out by the boxful and as a result, I have been left with absolutely nothing to buy in the clothing department. Now, the fact that I see this as anything close to a negative may seem inconsistent since I'm billing the kid for everything but there are certain things you really just want to buy and some of those things are adorable, sweet, tiny baby outfits. It's ridiculous how much fun it is to go into one of those outrageously overpriced boutiques and get totally scammed by a snooty saleswoman (who has no children) looking to bilk you for a hundred dollars in return for an outfit that will be worn exactly two times—once when you put it on the child and it's too big and then again when you put it on the child and it's too small.

I have made an arrangement with Lucie and Bing by way of their mothers. I get to be overindulgent with their birthday presents and get them whatever I want—really swell outfits—because eventually, they'll end up in Callie's closet. Thus, there's no need to feel I've gone overboard. I get my rocks off in the shopping department and several small people get cool clothes.

Now it seems perfectly clear to me that Callie should cover those costs as she is basically getting a full wardrobe in return for these few tokens of appreciation. Therefore, I submit the following for reimbursement. On the occasion of Lucie's second birthday, she received a very sweet dress and a really cute pant and cardigan outfit.

QTY/ITEM	CAT	PRICE	TOTAL
1 Dress	gift	36.00	
1 Pant	gift	30.00	
1 Cardigan	gift	36.00	
		$102.00	$3,949.11

Regarding the crib — it appears it will be delivered over the first weekend in June. I am glad for the crib and basically unbothered by the natural vs. white issue. However, I am very conflicted about the rest of what this all means. With the arrival of the crib comes also the reality that my baby is outgrowing her cradle. She is fast approaching the moment when she should begin to sleep in her new, big crib in her own room and not in her bassinet pulled tightly up against my bed so that my hand can rest on her sleeping body. This time is nearly at an end.

I am not so keen on that.

May 22 — Tuesday

Just cleaned out my wallet and found a few receipts. It's an odd assortment but all justifiable. Diapers go on the tally without question as do medical expenses not covered by insurance.

As for the soundtrack to *Oh Brother Where Art Thou* — well, "You Are My Sunshine" is Callie's favorite song and it's the third track on the CD. The song works like magic when she won't stop crying with anything else. But even she was getting tired of me just singing the chorus over and over. We needed to get all the words and now we have them thanks to the CD.

QTY/ITEM	CAT	PRICE	TOTAL
1 PMP BBYFR ALOE	diapers	5.99	
Hospital charge	medical	20.80	
Doctor charge	medical	10.00	
Vitamins	endless medical	15.99	
1 CD/*Oh Brother Where Art Thou*	noise abatement	18.89	
		$71.67	$4,020.78

I must also recognize a credit. As a mother, I am now eligible (as noted earlier) for an entirely new holiday and, subsequently, its gifts. My mother, for Mother's Day, covered the costs of my impatiens (and also held the baby while I planted them in the yard).

QTY/ITEM	CAT	PRICE	TOTAL
1 Credit	Mother's Day	+ $50.00	($550.00)

May 23 — Wednesday

We are taking shifts. I take the morning, until 1 P.M. when Mom shows up. She's on the clock until 3 P.M. Then Lonnie takes over and walks the walk until 6 P.M. Then I'm back on patrol. Of course, it's up to me to be there for feedings every two hours, or every hour as she has been so inclined today. But other than that, the day is mine—except for those days when this plan doesn't work with one of the other's schedule and except for the nineteen hours that I'm on. But I'm not resentful. Do I sound it? I'm not. I actually had a moment today when I focused on something other than baby desires—though oddly I cannot tell you what it is that I focused on. I'm sure it was something worthwhile; I'm just not sure what.

This is all in preparation. We are on the countdown to reentry, my return to work. And here it is again, great support for the tally, the teaching of fiscal responsibility. Would I leave my baby for anything less than the almighty dollar? No. Would I leave her for the almighty dollar? Yes. Sorry for that sad reality check but so would you. We have to. There is no other choice. I must make the living to avoid the dying.

I make my living in a number of ways—some of them are retrievable at this point and some are not. First is my three days a week in the offices of Scholastic Inc., where I create, build, and execute contests for the children of America. I will return to this work come the middle of June. For these days, I must exchange my daughter for a train ticket into Grand Central Station. I will be two hours away from her for twelve-hour stretches. To say I'm freaked out about this is to understate the

emotion. I can't really think about it right now. I can only prepare for it in little steps.

Second is my career as an actress making TV commercials.
Even if I am able to figure out how I will manipulate this babyland schedule to allow me to make the endless inane last-
minute one-minute auditions that take place in the city that are
necessary to book inane thirty-second commercials, I cannot
show up in my present condition. I am thirty-five pounds away
from commercialism and that ain't comin' off without steady
babyless breaks to jog the same incessant two-mile route up
and back, sweating and panting and hating every step.

Finally, there are my freelance writing jobs wherein I write
such enduring classics as *Pokemon Chapter Book #11: The Four
Star Challenge, Powerpuff Girls Chapter Book #6: Party Savers*, and
Scooby-Doo: You-Solve-It Super Sleuth Book. For these assign-
ments I simply need time at the keyboard (and of course, an ice
pick to lobotomize myself in order to become appropriately
submerged in the material involved).

It's a diverse and somewhat troubled career and not perhaps the one I dreamt of, but it's mine. I've diligently carved it
out over the last many years and the bottom line is this—with
all these components going strong, I make a rather nice living.
Without them all, it gets dodgy. It appears to me that we are in
for a few dodgy days as the demands of babyland make time
hard to find, fat tough to lose, and distance a sadness not worth
exploring.

The looming question is this: loss of livelihood—do I bill
for it?

May 24 — Thursday

My baby had a terrible day yesterday. She had to go to the doctor for two more shots, another Hepatitis B and a Polio vaccine.

She's too smart. I laid her on the examining table and got one snap unsnapped before she locked eyes and looked at me with authentic terror. It was less than a second later before she was on top of a full-scale wail; a really, really loud scream that even got Dr. Brown to look on in amazement. Callie was completely petrified. She has never grabbed anything in her life. I have been baiting her with rattles and shiny things but at this point, she hadn't reached for anything. But now, suddenly, she was grabbing me, first with her tiny fist on my sleeve and then with her whole arm wrapped around mine. Her communication was completely clear: "You're supposed to save me! So *save me!*"

It was horrible. It took a double-breasted feeding in the back room just to calm down enough to leave the office.

And today, we're still recovering from the trauma of it all. It's left me feeling weepy and bent on sweet thoughts of my girl. I want to say nice things about her and so I was just about to espouse the financial glories of babyhood. I was ready to wax on about how little money I've actually spent since her arrival. I was on the verge of glorifying how economical she is with her breast-feeding ways and her delight in the simple things of life, mirrors and crinkly things, and the wonders of rocking. It has struck me that she does not ask for an entertainment budget and I wanted to let her now how much I appreciate that.

In reality, once her room was set up and the basic components were purchased, she hasn't cost much. Okay. Diapers. She's a bit of a diaper whore but other than that—and I suppose a few doctor co-pays and maybe the odd bottle of Infant Tylenol here and there—but really, it hasn't been much. Then the mail came.

She got mail. She has been invited to her first birthday party. My reaction is mixed: I think it's fabulous that she's been invited since who doesn't want a popular baby? And I'm delighted that Callie's presence has been requested at the celebration of one young Olivia Bowman's third birthday. But while I'm not suggesting this one invitation alone will be our undoing, it has opened the door in my mind to a whole new world of expense—gifts for friends, gifts for family, gifts in appreciation, and gifts for influence. In essence, gifts are a basic cost of doing business as a baby.

Because, of course, she must arrive at this fete with a fabulous present because that's what babies of her caliber are called upon to do. I do not want to suggest to her that she must buy her way into social circles because clearly she has received this first invitation due only to her sweet countenance and because she lives nearby. But still, it is important to make a good first impression.

One must be selective and gracious when choosing a gift—must truly give the perfect gift, whatever that may be, regardless of expense because it's about generosity of spirit and not economy. I do not know what we will decide upon. I suspect that a three-year-old would be far more impressed with a kick-ass toy as opposed to a ridiculously cute new outfit so perhaps we should get her both. Or neither. Perhaps we should buy her a pony. Okay. Not a pony but still, something truly swell. We will go shopping in the next few days and figure it out.

It hadn't occurred to me until now that even a baby must keep up with the Joneses. Color me shallow if you must but I believe I speak a truth.

May 27 — Sunday

QTY/ITEM	CAT	PRICE	TOTAL
1 Gerb NUK nwbn 2510	nipple replacement	$3.39	$4,024.17

A good nipple is hard to find. I never realized that until recently. One of the many business ideas I have had since Callie's arrival is this—make a damn nipple that *really* replicates the real thing. I first thought of this when it appeared my own nipples might be in danger of exploding from pain about six weeks ago and I wasn't allowed to give the babe a bottle due to nipple confusion. God forbid she take milk from one of those latex imposters and then forget how to feed from the real thing.

Nipple confusion—it's one of the major fears of early childhood and modern man.

So, tell me this, how is it possible in this new millennium in which we are living, where moon walking is old news, sheep that were never born are roaming the earth, and an entire world that doesn't exist actually does exist in a place called cyber—how is it possible that we haven't come up with a nipple that's not confusing?

I ask this question again now as we are baby stepping our

way toward my return to work and Callie must learn to take nourishment and solace from a bottle topped with confusion. I have been pumping my guts out in the middle of the night and on off-hours, straining to produce enough extra leche to have the contents necessary for our teaching bottles. I can't tell you the heartache I feel when she rejects the bottle and I have to dump the reheated stuff down the drain.

In an effort to avoid more of this painful rejection, we have tried every commercially available nipple without much success. I mentioned to my mother this notion of a nipple that truly replicates the real thing. I said I would pay big money for such an item. A hundred dollars? Whatever. Would it need a hydrolic lift or space-age plasti-materials? Okay. Just give me the damn nipple.

Mom said, "Do you suppose such a thing exists?"

"I think we would have heard about it in all our research, don't you?"

"I suppose," she said, "but what about like the mahariji or something?"

"No," I answered. "They use other people. You don't need to buy nipples when you can afford the whole person."

Mom nodded and we rocked on in silence.

Later, she heard from a cousin whose "boob-addicted" grandchildren have had the greatest luck with the NUK nipple. Good enuk, I say.

We have purchased a set of two with high hopes.

I also purchased a few other things while at CVS, much of it in the absorbent family. We are a very leaky household.

QTY/ITEM	CAT	PRICE	TOTAL
1 68-pack Pampers Stretch	sanitation	12.79	
1 Evenflo nurse pads	basic decency	6.29	
1 Vitamin refill	maternal maintenance	15.99	
		$35.07	$4,059.24

May 29 — Tuesday

QTY/ITEM	CAT	PRICE	TOTAL
1 Prosobee RTU — formula	grocery	$7.19	$4,066.43

We have purchased Olivia a Sprinkle'n'Sparkle Paint Your Own Umbrella Art Kit. We also got her a lovely cat bracelet that will adorn the outside of her gift. We are pleased with the art kit even though the package recommends that only children five and above paint their own umbrellas. Callie and I are confident that Olivia, with the help of her mother, is easily advanced enough to handle the task. The package is wrapped in a very lively balloon-decorated paper.

QTY/ITEM	CAT	PRICE	TOTAL
1 Sprinkle'n' Sparkle Umbrella Kit	gifts	19.95	
1 Wooden cat bracelet	gifts	5.50	
		$25.45	$4,091.88

It is not a wildly expensive gift but it is tasteful and fun-filled and it will, I am confident, receive an enthusiastic response when unveiled, which will reflect well on the baby.

Now that the "gift" door has been opened, I am seeing the fuller ramifications—Christmas and birthdays for the entire family will now mean that in addition to the impossible task of finding the perfect gift from me, I will also be searching for the perfect gift from an infant who refuses to shop for herself. This is an expense of both time and money though, of course, I will only charge Callie for the actual cost of the item selected.

To that end, Grandpa's birthday is around the corner and I have not had a moment for the kind of free-form image association it takes to come up with a gift for the man who has whatever the hell he wants when he wants it. Dad doesn't tend to wait for holidays and when he shops he shops hard. He buys the best and the brightest. It's tough to keep up.

So I've taken the old "kid cop-out"—photographs. I remember even as a small child feeling like I was really pulling a fast one when I would wrap up a school photograph in its cardboard frame and call it Christmas for my grandparents. In return they would pack the Cadillac to the brim and rent a small trailer in order to deliver my Christmas. The inequity was clear and yet, when they opened those Christmas pictures, the reaction they gave—you would have thought it was the Hope diamond. So, what the hell, it worked then, it should work now.

To be honest, I'm gliding on the kid's coattails. "We" are giving a gift so I'm basically using Callie as a cover.

We will split the cost of the frames I bought though. Which, I must tell you, still makes for a very inexpensive gift, as the child appears to have something of a knack for bargains. We went to purchase two frames, one for Grandpa's picture and one for her fine hospital certificate, which just arrived in the mail. When I presented the frames to the cashier, I was informed that there was a one-time-only two-for-one deal.

Her spendthrift nature showed itself again the other day when her father borrowed a quarter from her to make a phone call. (Okay. It was my quarter but she was holding my wallet, which is her way, tucked in beside her in her car seat.) When Lonnie returned from the pay phone he handed the child two quarters. (Okay. He didn't hand them to her because she can't hold things yet but the point is—he came back with two quarters.) It seems that not only was the number he tried to call busy but the pay phone returned two coins for the one.

She might have a gift.

I'd like to think some of this is my doing. The universe appears to be buffering Callie from economic hardship. Could it be that the universe is aware she has a mother who is charging her for her very existence? Perhaps. And in exchange for her unfortunate burden, the universe has decided it will comp whatever items it can.

QTY/ITEM	CAT	PRICE	TOTAL
1 Saratoga 4x6 frame	gifts	4.99	
1 Wellington 8x10 frame (50%)	gifts	4.49	
		_____	
		$4.49	$4,096.37

June 1 — Friday

QTY/ITEM	CAT	PRICE	TOTAL
1 Credit	internment rebate	+ 92.00	($642.00)
1 Pampers Baby Fresh Wipes	sanitation	6.59	
1 Pampers Stretch	sanitation	12.79	
		_____	
		$19.38	$4,115.75

I think it's time to address the issue of insurance—if for no other reason than I am trying to bury my brain in some consuming activity so I do not hear the screeching painful cries of my baby as her grandmother attempts to give her a bottle of formula. This is the third day for formula and it's not going well. Yesterday, Callie finally took a few ounces but only when I gave in, took her from Gramma, and offered her the bottle myself. As delighted as I may be that the girl took some sustenance, the point of this exercise is that she must learn to take it from others as I soon must journey to that New City of York in order to make us the money we need to tide us over until she can repay me.

I cannot stay in the room while she's howling. It will only end in my grabbing her away from my mother and soothing her and ultimately putting us all back to square one.

Damn! She's loud. She's a very loud baby.

I really don't want to go all the way back to the beginning of the insurance issue. I do not want to relive being deeply nauseous in the first days of pregnancy and fighting with the idiot from the insurance company who insisted they would not put my OB-GYN in network because there was an in-network doctor in my area.

When I pointed out that that doctor happened to be a podiatrist, the customer-service specialist on the other end of the phone replied, "I know you may think that doesn't make sense."

I confirmed his suspicions.

My insurance had been, up to that point, provided by the Screen Actors Guild thanks to my modest success as a commercial actress. I had the option of coverage through Scholastic but had always declined it as it seemed silly to pay for a second coverage. Now, however, it appeared that the small bi-weekly hit on the paycheck for Scholastic's coverage would be minimal compared to the amount my other insurance wouldn't cover.

I know this is an embarrassment of riches in a country where so many are completely uninsured but the really sick thing is that at this point I now have two complete insurance plans but am still paying some of my medical costs.

There is no other way to explain it—it's a fucked-up business.

I opted not to bill Callie for the addition of a second insurance plan for a couple of reasons. One, I will benefit from the additional coverage on doctor visits and medical costs that do not involve her and two, I cannot put the whole of the failed Clinton health plan on her tiny shoulders. In a few years, when she's older, we will discuss the possibilities available to solve the health crisis in America and perhaps at that point, should she be unable to come up with a viable solution, I may bill her retroactively. But at present, with no command of the English language, it seems unfair.

I do feel it is absolutely fair and proper, however, that she should be billed for the increase in deductions from my paycheck that I have experienced since her birth. That is, she should pay for the bi-weekly cost of her own coverage. Since I am behind in this regard, I will record all payments to date.

QTY/ITEM	CAT	PRICE	TOTAL
5 HMO Aetna US Healthcare premium @ $15.29	insurance	76.45	
5 Dental PPO @ $3.90	insurance	19.50	
5 Vision @ $4.54	insurance	22.70	
		$118.65	$4,234.40

I know it might seem silly to sign her up for dental already since she doesn't have any teeth. But I was afraid I might forget in a year or two and suddenly be dentorily screwed. Okay. Perhaps she should not pay for my OCD neurosis.

QTY/ITEM	CAT	PRICE	TOTAL
1 Credit—Dental	OCD	+ $19.50	($661.50)

June 4—Monday

Days like this—it seems impossible that there's absolutely nothing for which I can bill her. I would like to. I would like to have something to show for my worn body. But I went through my wallet twice looking for some kind of receipt and there isn't a thing.

Callie made her maiden voyage into the big city today. She rode MetroNorth for free and was simply lifted over the turnstile in the subway. She didn't eat a hot dog, order anything at Dean & Deluca, or purchase herself one of those green foam Statue of Liberty hats. Her debut in the big town and at the office to meet all my workmates was thus completely free of expense. And yet, I am depleted, weaker than I was, beaten down, and broken. It is unfair that such a state is totally unbillable.

Here's the thing about my girl—she sleeps through the night, which denies me sympathy from most other parents, but the flip side to that happy equation is that she does not sleep during the day, save the occasional catnap, and today she didn't even take one of those. But do not be fooled. This is not to say that she remains awake and bubbling with joyful gurgles and toothless grins. No, I'm afraid not.

She becomes the demonic baby, the one we call . . . Sally. We don't really know Sally, don't know where she comes from, don't know where she goes when she leaves. We only know that when Sally is here, we don't have fun.

Sally is awake all the time and filled, apparently, with an ungodly amount of gas and other flotsam. When Sally appears, there is only one thing I can do (and I do mean "I" because Gramma, Dad, nobody else works when Sally shows up. She's a persnickety, demanding little cur and if there's any chance of her going silent for even a moment, it has to be Mom at the wheel. This is one of the reasons my mom says that God likes men more.) Anyway, when Sally possesses my beautiful baby's body, the child demands movement, constant movement. All the time. All day. She's a movement junkie, Sally is, and we're not talking gentle jiggles and sways. No. She demands deep knee bends and fully extended arm swings, the kind that wear away those pads between your bones and snap tendons that thought they were done moving that way a few years ago.

I have this idea for a workout tape: a collection of exercises done while holding a baby wherein the baby is trainer—a kick-ass trainer. The knee bends aren't deep enough? Don't burn enough? The baby cries. If the baby cries, you aren't doing it right. Swing her up and back with fully extended arms. If she cries, you're not stretching enough. Whatever the exercise, if you aren't deep enough into the pain of it, your baby trainer will wail one of those screeching howls that burns through protective clothing and sails right down to the very base of your spine, stealing sleep and your sense of well-being and forcing you to respond like some kind of indentured servant—anything to make it stop. Anything. I bounce through entire episodes of *Law & Order.* I sway even when someone else is holding her, unconsciously praying it will keep her from crying. Just don't cry. Please don't cry.

I will either be very toned or dead inside of a year—probably dead since my best efforts have achieved very little in the way of weight loss. This stuff on my body is like some new, improved version of fat that doesn't scrub, melt, or chip off. It's a baked-on mess.

Which brings me to this—I think the baby is accelerating my aging process. I'm grayer than I was, of that I am sure. But more than that, my knees are going and the back is sending out warning signs. There is an ache in my joints that makes me walk in such a way that I find myself thinking of my grandfather. With this constant motion, I should be thin by now and not living in terror with regards to dealing with my agent and my lack of commercial appeal.

I thought kids were supposed to keep you young. I thought they were supposed to bring you back around full circle to see the world as you once did, fresh and new. Well, I am beginning to suspect that is not true because at this rate, I'm going to be looking at the world from over the top of a very big walker and I don't remember that from my childhood.

Callie is sucking the youth right out of me and it's showing up on her, looking way better than it's looked on me for a very long time.

But there's no way to bill her for that.

June 5 — Tuesday

I hear crying in the woods. When I'm out jogging along the Appalachian Trail, I hear it. Perhaps it is the Old Crying Baby of

Appalachia or perhaps not, because I hear crying other places, too. Sometimes I hear crying when Callie is asleep in my arms.

And so today, I purchased some things to stop her from crying.

QTY/ITEM	CAT	PRICE	TOTAL
1 Avent bottle warmer	lunch security	46.99	
1 Boppy neck ring	head security	5.99	
4 Gymini toy attachments	mom security*	14.98	
1 Pair blue socks	fashion security**	3.00	
		$70.96	$4,305.36

*Okay, these are sort of for me since I'm bored out of my mind with the current three toys. Callie, on the other hand, hasn't even gotten to them yet.

**Obviously, blue socks all on their own will not stop Callie's crying but it will help coordinate her outfits again since we lost one of her other blue socks in the laundry last week. Since no one really knows why a baby cries—who's to say it isn't a cry against fashion faux pas?

When I finished my shopping, I returned my agent's latest phone call.

He said, "Hey . . . how are you?"

I said, "I'm good. How are you?"

He said, "I'm great. Listen, I just felt like you fell into that deep dark hole of 'She was going to have a baby,' 'Did she have the baby?' 'She had the baby,' 'Has anyone heard from her since the baby?' thing and I just wanted to check in with you to see what was going on."

"Well, actually—the thing is I'm still in that black hole of 'I've had the baby and now I'm too fat to do commercials' thing."

He laughed and said he completely got it. (Please God that he meant it and someday I will actually book a commercial again and go to the post office and find one of those lovely pink checks from my agent's office whereupon I commence to doin' the pinkie dance right there in the post office with the post-office people watching.) I hemmed and hawed and finally begged off another month (as if I'm really going to lose thirty-five pounds in a month). And, I also told him I'd be willing to go out on mother/daughter calls with Callie until she was conscious and could understand the world was way too focused on her. Of course, I didn't mention why—that she owes me a fair sum and it would be an easy way for her to pay me back.

Then he asked, "Would it help you to know that your agent has put on a few pounds, too?"

"No," I told him. "But thanks for trying."

June 6 — Wednesday

Today I am thirty-nine years old. Callie is twelve weeks. For my birthday, she gave me a visit to the pediatrician's office. We have three areas of concern: 1. She has, over the last week, developed a rasp in her voice (read: her wail) that makes her sound like Brenda Vaccaro, 2. She seems to be less than enthralled with her one-bottle-a-day of soy formula to the extent that this afternoon when I took a deep breath and left her with Dad and Gramma and drove off to the train station to pick up Tory, who needed a post-wrist-surgery lift home, Callie opted to wail for the seventy-five minutes I was away instead of eat

the food that was offered. And, further and on that same subject perhaps but I'm not sure, she appears to be having a bit of
trouble with her daily constitution (read: seven constitutions),
and 3. The girl will not sleep during the day at all and is therefore exhausted (read: I'm exhausted) and I believe that this is
an overriding factor in numbers 1 and 2.

Of course, as soon as we arrived at Dr. Brown's office, she
fell asleep.

Dr. Brown said it's a given in his field that those sickest at
home will be finest in his office and those finest at home will be
sickest for him and therefore, a baby who simply will not sleep
during the day is certain to pass out at 4 P.M. in front of him
and that's how he knows she's not sleeping otherwise. Or
something like that.

For my birthday, the doctor used the "c" word. Colic.

I said, "But isn't it late for that? Shouldn't she have come up
with that sooner if she was going to go through it?" I could feel
a panic rising up in me, the thought of having one of those god-
forsaken colicky babies, as if putting that name on it made the
crying I've already endured any worse. It shouldn't but it does.

The doc said, "No. The time is just about right—two to
three months."

"And how long does it last?"

"About two to three months." And then he looked at me
with a sort of sympathy that I am not accustomed to. I'm the
one with the exceptionally beautiful baby who is clearly brilliant and alert and who sleeps through the night. People can
look at me with envy—but don't look at me with sympathy.
Please. It can only mean what's coming is going to hurt.

"I can only say to you," the doc continued, "it will get better."

"It's really not that bad on *me*." I wanted to set him straight, make him see that this is not colic, just a baby with a raspy voice due to a cold and exhausted due to the fact that she is so brilliantly alert that she refuses to sleep during the day. It's not colic. "I just feel bad for *her*," I told him. "So what about the Brenda Vaccaro voice?"

"I'd say she's hoarse from screaming so much."

"You didn't hear any congestion when you listened to her chest?"

"She sounded fine," he said and began to explain the vast array of avenues down which we could walk to determine colic from acid reflux from god knows what else.

"I really don't want to get into a lot of drugs and medical procedures yet," I told him in response to his litany of gastric options.

"Right," he said, "so we'll start with switching to a milk-based formula. And, though we don't like to drug babies, you could try a quarter teaspoon of Benadryl to help her sleep."

A battle rose up in me—between horror that the doctor might suggest tranquilizing my sweet baby girl and relief that he had given me permission to dose her out of our screaming, sleepless misery.

Me—sister to a heroin addict, widely related to a number of alcoholics, and with a personal history (read: fondness) for a variety of powders, pills, and liquids—I went home and gave my baby Benadryl.

She's sleeping now.

QTY/ITEM	CAT	PRICE	TOTAL
1 Doctor's visit	co-pay	15.00	
1 Benadryl, Dye-Free	baby narcotic	5.99	
1 Enfamil (milk-based)	laxative	7.99	
1 Brach's spice drops	mother pacifier	1.49	
		$30.47	$4,335.83

June 7 — Thursday

QTY/ITEM	CAT	PRICE	TOTAL
1 *Dr. Ferber's Solve Your Child's Sleep Problems*	R&R	$10.79	$4,346.62

June 9 — Saturday

I have come up with another business idea that I offer up to Callie free of charge as a way to earn the monies necessary to pay me back for her expenses: Mom Food.

I believe there is a real need in the marketplace for a line of foods that is parent-friendly; that is to say, food that can be opened and eaten with one hand while not endangering the infant balanced in the other. Some will be frozen, some not, but all of them will be meals and snacks created in such a way that they can be prepared and eaten with one hand and no napkin; if you wipe your hands clean on your clothes, whatever comes off on the material should be guaranteed to come out in the wash. This suggests that there should be no grease, which is in keeping with the fact that these meals and snacks must be economically caloried, that is to say they cannot make the fat mom any fatter.

This line of food could also be used by amputees but the marketing would be primarily to parents as, like it or not, it just makes for a prettier commercial.

June 10 — Sunday

QTY/ITEM	CAT	PRICE	TOTAL
1 pmp prm jmb sz 1*	sanitation	$13.49	$4,366.11

*For the unindoctrinated: Pampers Premium, Jumbo, Size 1

Subj: To the very generous in my life
Date: 6/11 (Monday)
Dear Hand-Me-Downers:

Okay—believe it or not—the time has come that even Miss Callie has hand-me-downs to offer up to the world. The child is now two feet tall and well beyond many of her earliest outfits. Therefore, it is also time to discuss hand-me-down protocol and etiquette.

Since you have all been very generous with your hand-me-downs, I want to be sure I handle the further disbursement of said articles according to your wishes. (I have spoken to some of you about this but your response to this inquiry will act as the official confirmation of your *wishes.) Here's my question for the lot of you—do you want anything back? If so, do you know which items?*

I don't actually think any of this very early stuff came from you folks but it's clear things will be coming and going at a goodly pace now that the child has truly grasped all the nuances of eating and is practicing her skill often and with abandon, something akin to a Hoover, and therefore will be tossing off your offerings in no time flat. Once she has done so, I feel it's only right that Miss Callie should pass along her savings to other babies as your babies have passed it along to her—assuming this economic plan meets with your approval. Should it come to pass that any of the items in question are sold through tag, stoop, yard, or barn sale, we will certainly split the net proceeds with you.

Let me know your feelings and I will sort and purge in accordance.
With great appreciation,
Betsy & Callie

June 12—Tuesday

Here ends my baby's first fiscal quarter.

They grow up so fast.

We have plans to celebrate her upcoming 100-day birthday. I will not be billing her for a single plastic fork. This party is on me—fully comped—because she deserves to be celebrated.

But before we can celebrate, we must do a final first quarter tally:

QTY/ITEM	CAT	PRICE	TOTAL
1 4-pack Enfamil	groceries	$7.99	$4,368.10

Please join us as we salute
our new Commander in Chief
on the occasion of her

First 100 Days in Office*

Saturday, June 25
5:00 P.M.
RSVP
Regrets only
No gifts–please

*That is to say, Betsy and Lonnie would very much like you to stop by for a drink and a chat and we're using Callie's 100-day birthday as the reason since she's done a lot more to improve our quality of life than that other Commander in Chief.

Credits: $661.50
Disbursements: $4,368.10

The Second
Fiscal Quarter

~

Parent Company

June 18 — Monday

5:00 to 6:00 A.M.	Breast-feed
6:00 A.M.	Betsy out of bed
	Callie still in bed
6:15 A.M.	Betsy leaves for NYC
7:30 to 8:30 A.M.	Breast milk bottle (up to 3 ozs)
	Offer in 1.5-oz portions
	Diaper change
	Clothing change (essential)
	Sleep?
	It will probably be 3 hours before next feeding.

8:49 A.M.	Lonnie calls Mom—decide on shift-change time
11:30 A.M. (ish)	Formula bottle (4 ozs)
2:00 P.M. (ish)	Breast milk bottle (3 ozs)
	Could give Benadryl prior to feeding to encourage nap
4:30 to 5:00 P.M. (ish)	Formula bottle (4 ozs)
7:00 P.M. (ish)	Hopefully, I'm back in time for this feeding
	If not, a breast milk bottle

I left Callie with her father, both of them peaceful and asleep, almost an hour and a half ago to take this train into the city. And now, I really don't have any idea how she is and it's making me nuts. I don't know if she's still sleeping or if she's awake and happily taking a bottle from Dad or if she woke up and didn't see me next to her and freaked. She might be sad right now and I can't do anything about it. Or she might be absolutely blissful but I don't know.

And that makes me feel like I want to puke. I just want to get to the end of this day.

They turn you into great big clichés, that's what babies do. They take perfectly good women filled with their own questions and conquests and conflicts and confidences (me, for example) and they turn them into worrying, weepy, wistful, wondering blobs. We are those thick-torsoed people who run in and out of grocery stores continually distracted. You can look at us and imagine that this is not us looking our best, that once we probably looked pretty good but things have gotten away from us, been forgotten since then, put on the back burner. We are focused completely on that baby in the cart or stroller or sling or in the arms and that doesn't leave room in our brains to think about our hair. There is really nothing else, only those things that can be worked into the baby's schedule. All other schedules have bitten the dust. And to stray from that notion leaves you vulnerable to high anxiety and a deep-seated nausea.

All I want to do is get on the cell phone, call home, get the blow-by-blow report on absolutely every move the baby has made since my departure. But of course I can't do that because that would be just too predictable. Besides, I might wake her up and that would make me a bad mom.

But I want to know—is she sleeping on her side or on her back? Does she have her head tilted up and to the side or is it tucked in with her nose just below the blanket trim? Has she smiled yet this morning?

Does she miss me?

June 19—Tuesday

Callie, apparently, did not miss me. She was blissful and giggly all day.

We don't need to go into the various double-edged emotions that this news brings up in me but come on, you'd think she could have at least freaked out a little—just at the beginning— just for a minute. Would that have been so hard?

But of course, we cannot acknowledge this dark side of Mommy. We must be delighted that the baby is so well-adjusted that she is perfectly fine when Mommy just disappears. Off the face of the earth for all she knows, but does she cry? Does she kick? No!

Okay. Baby is happy and baby is good. So, in celebration

of a very successful first day away from each other, Callie and I went shopping today. And I'm charging her for every last dime.

From Kmart:

QTY/ITEM	CAT	PRICE	TOTAL
1 Ortho nipple	confusion reduction	1.99	
1 Pamper Baby Dry	sanitation	11.97	
1 8-pack AA batteries	breast pump security	7.97	
1 4-pack D batteries	Graco swing security	5.99	
		$27.92	$4,396.02

From BJ's Wholesale Club:

QTY/ITEM	CAT	PRICE	TOTAL
1 Pampers giant	extended sanitation	28.59	
1 Ken's mayo Xtra Lg*	Father's Day/gifts	3.99	
1 Jet basketball	Father's Day/gifts	14.99	
		$47.57	$4,443.59

Daddy is a mayo freak. This is the sense of humor gift that accompanies the serious gift of a basketball.

2 Enfamil	groceries	15.98	
1 Sassy Pacifier Keeper	pacifier management	3.99	

continued on next page

continued from previous page			
1 Baby Pacifier NUK	replacement	2.99	
1 Brachs Spice Drops	mom management	1.49	
		$24.45	$4,468.04

June 20 — Wednesday

Here's the good news for the day. It seems the powers that be at Scholastic would like me to continue my leave until the end of the summer, whereupon the new building will finally be open and I will have my own cubicle. That is to say, while I was away, they gave away my desk.

Cause for paranoia? Perhaps. But I stay calm. I am a rock.

Okay, I say, sounds doable.

Except, they say, it's not really a "leave" because we want you to work from home.

Okay, I say. Of course, I've never tried to do real work while attached to a three-month-old but . . . okay.

Good. So we'll just see you once a week for meetings.

Okie-dokie.

So here's the new schedule, Lonnie takes the angel from 10 A.M. until noon, Mom handles her from noon until 2 P.M. Whereupon, I damn well better be sure I have my work done because she's back in my court then.

It's hard to juggle a lot of balls all at once. As any clown worth her salt will tell you, it's even harder to juggle several things of different sizes and shapes. And I have come to understand that a baby, a job, freelance work, and laundry are all very different shapes.

June 22 — Friday

Today, my baby is one hundred days old.

My friend, Jo, who lives in Tokyo with her husband and her eight-month-old baby, passed along some wisdom to me early on in Callie's life.

She said that the old people in her country have a saying — it professes that with a newborn child, you must have one hundred days of patience.

And so, on this day, I have and she is and it is better now. She is so very completely present and accounted for now that I believe soon she will be able to seek employment.

June 23 — Saturday

Callie's party, though expensive and unbillable (that would be gauche), was a fine affair. And even though the summer storms hung a thickness in the air that Miss Callie can't tolerate in good grace and, in addition, it appears that her gums are somewhat on fire due to budding teeth (good thing I got the dental), I would say our guests were delighted and bemused by the guest of honor.

That said, I am beginning to question the validity of the "one hundred days of patience." Dr. Brown says teething is possible now — early but possible — and when I mentioned having heard she could be teething and yet still not get a tooth for several months he said yes, that, too, sadly, is also possible. As a result of teething and being transitioned from her cradle to her crib, she is beginning an in-depth study of odd numbers, that is 1(A.M), 3(A.M.), 5(A.M.), 7(A.M.). And her crying, slobbering, and chew-crazy machinations are begging more patience than ever before—along with the purchase of any and all items that offer up hope, however small, of relief—for all of us.

QTY/ITEM	CAT	PRICE	TOTAL
1 Baby teether beads	noise reduction	2.49	
1 Baby teether Pooh	option 2	4.99	
1 Baby teether Nuk	option 3	1.99	
1 Baby Orajel	drugs	5.99	
		$15.46	$4,483.50

And while we're at it, a few more charges:

QTY/ITEM	CAT	PRICE	TOTAL
1 Evenflo nurse pads	absorbtion	6.29	
1 Aetna US Healthcare co-pay	insurance	15.29	
1 Vision @ $4.54	insurance	4.54	
		$26.12	$4,509.62

As for the value of things—let us, for a moment, discuss what price one can put on the value of having Gramma on hand.

In the midst of the party, my neighbor Sara wandered upstairs to see Callie's nursery, whereupon she found Gramma and granddaughter deeply involved in a bottle.

Sara said, "She is just unbelievably beautiful."

Mom/Gramma looked up at her and with total sincerity said, "Thank you for being honest."

June 24—Sunday

QTY/ITEM	CAT	PRICE	TOTAL
1 Offering	soul redemption	$5.00	$4,514.62

I haven't been to church in twenty years and don't really intend to pick it up now but I do think that Callie should go for reasons that sound truly trite and obvious when I speak them aloud.

They begin and end with Gramma. Gramma goes to church. She's big on it. Says it does her good. But she's so new to things around here that I didn't feel it proper to merely point her in the right direction and shove her out the door. It's only right that I accompany her during this introductory phase. And, that means coughing up a little cash for the offering dish since, after all, I am taking up pew space—plenty of it, too.

The point is, eventually someone will have to take Callie to Sunday School and I don't know that I'm the one for the job. So I'll go with them to get the ball rolling and once Mom is comfortable, I'll send them off on their own. Mom gets such a kick out of it anyway that it simply makes good sense that the two of them should go off each and every Sunday morning, get a little righteousness for their souls, a few doughnuts for their bellies, and enough rules and regulations that when it comes time to rebel, Callie will have plenty to work with and won't end up diving into the deep end of a pool with no water. Let her personal counterculture movement have less to do with the counter and more to do with the culture. That is, I don't want—when it comes time for her to reach out to push away— for her to thrust out her fist and find no resistance. Force against a void, it's a recipe for instability. You're sure to fall down.

I'll have her dressed and ready to go by 8:30 every Sunday morning. It'll be fun dressing up in church clothes—and here's my deal—I won't even bill her for them, only the offering. The togs, they'll be on me. That's my arrangement with God.

June 29 — Friday

QTY/ITEM	CAT	PRICE	TOTAL
1 Credit	internment rebate	+ $81.00	($742.50)

I believe this rebate credit is soon coming to the end of its line. I have been rearranged once again by the powers-that-be at Scholastic. Beginning next week, I will be going to the city twice a week and that will most likely dig a deep hole into the child's rebate even if she continues to hold me prisoner on the days when I am home.

I am not looking forward to twice a week. These NYC days are bad for my glands. No matter how much I use my handy-dandy breast pump, I feel like Dolly Parton by the end of the day. In fact, the pump seems to exacerbate the situation so that by the time I get off the train and into my car to drive home, I must lean forward at a very particular angle so as not to allow the shoulder strap of my seat belt anywhere near my lactatious tatas.

I must say, I am finding myself less and less enamored by the inroads made through modern technology with regards to the perils and pitfalls of modern maternity.

QTY/ITEM	CAT	PRICE	TOTAL
1 Aetna US Healthcare co-pay	insurance	15.29	
1 Vision @ $4.54	insurance	4.54	
		$19.83	$4,534.45

July 1 — Sunday

QTY/ITEM	CAT	PRICE	TOTAL
1 Offering	continuing redemption	$5.00	$4,539.45

July 2 — Monday

Sally was here when I woke up this morning. She is a vile and heinous baby.

I resent her taking my child away with no authority to do so. I do not know what she does with Callie while she's here and I don't know if Callie is in on this little bait-and-switch but I am not amused. Sally has been crying and kicking since 6 A.M.

It is difficult, in these moments, to stay true to my intention here. Out of pure spite, I very much want to charge her an hourly rate for bad behavior but I cannot do so as this tally is only to serve as a log of actual expenses.

But if I could? She would owe me for five hours and that's just for today and the day is young, even if I am not.

It would be fun to come up with the hourly rate.

July 3 — Tuesday

Callie is becoming persnickety with regards to the breast. Now that she's a big shot with the bottle crowd, it appears she doesn't want to be seen with a breast in her mouth. This is the clearest indication to date that she has not yet grasped the value of a hard-earned buck. Therefore, the tally once again is proving to be justified. She has to learn, and where better than with milk money?

As far as Callie is concerned, breast is free, bottle is not. Breast milk is complimentary and comes with the flight but formula, formula not only costs, it costs dearly—nearly $8.00 per four-pack. But she doesn't appear to give a rat's ass about that. She likes the bottle life—gallivanting around showing off her big formula burps.

I've tried to talk to her about it, point up the value of a good tit, but she screams, kicks, and flails about like a cat on the way to the vet. In short, she is rejecting the breast in favor of the newer, more novel, easier-to-suck bottled option.

Modern times.

One might suspect I am simply hurt and experiencing the first in what will be an endless parade of rejection and separation at the hands of my little girl. It might be suggested that I am reacting in a bitter and spiteful manner with my talk of billing and expenses. It could also be said that I am not handling this well.

To which I say, "Yeah? So?"

July 4—Wednesday

One year ago today, I found out that Callie would be joining us. I saw fireworks.

July 5—Thursday

What to bill. What not to bill. This is getting trickier.

We're going to Chicago at the end of this month so the child can meet her paternal grandmother. This is not a trip I would take if Callie were not a factor. However, Lonnie travels there often. So I could pretty easily bill for my ticket and not Lonnie's and feel just fine about it.

However, come August, I'm planning to take Callie up to the cottage. The cottage is a house that sits on Lake Michigan. It was built the year I was born. I have spent time there every summer of my life. I want Callie to be able to say the same. Plus, I want Dad to see her again before she gets bigger. These are all Callie-related reasons but they are my wishes, not hers. So, do I bill? And what about the family wedding that's coming up in September? I would like to go as I'm very fond of the cousin being married but included in my decision-making is introducing Callie to the rest of the family. (I know that's not gracious as the wedding is obviously not about my child but on the other hand, everything is about my child. So there you have it. Those are the facts.) The point is, we're beginning to meld and I'm having trouble discerning what I want for me and what I want for her.

Would I go all these places in this time, in this way, if she were not here? Life is so changed from what it was just a year ago that I can't answer that question easily anymore. I don't know what I would have used to have done. I don't remember a "used to." Her existence has so thoroughly permeated the atmosphere that there is no sense of life without her here. There are no clear-cut lines anywhere.

QTY/ITEM	CAT	PRICE	TOTAL
2 Girl Fancy sock packs @ $4.99	style	9.98	
1 Babyseat rearview mirror	curiosity*	2.99	
4 Enfamil @ $7.99	breast R&R	31.96	
1 Pampers wipes	sanitation	5.99	
		$50.92	$4,590.37

My own. I've been wondering what she does back there while I'm driving.

July 6 — Friday

QTY/ITEM	CAT	PRICE	TOTAL
1 Aetna US Healthcare co-pay	insurance	15.29	
1 Vision @ $4.54	insurance	4.54	
		$19.83	$4,610.20

July 7 — Saturday

An advantage of returning to work above and beyond the pay-check, health coverage, and pension is girl talk. I mentioned to my friend Judy, who has two children, this notion I have that Callie is accelerating my aging process, the pained knees, aching shoulder, questionable back.

"That's just the fatigue," Judy says.

To which I reply, "Well, yes, perhaps, but then again, so is death—just fatigue of the most extreme nature. The final fatigue."

Perhaps I am a bit tired.

July 8 — Sunday

QTY/ITEM	CAT	PRICE	TOTAL
1 Offering	brimstone	$5.00	$4,615.20

July 9—Monday

Quiz time. What is this?

V-v-v-v-v-v-v-v-v, shzzzzzzz, v-v-v-v-v-v-v-v-v, shzzzzzzz, v-v-v-v-v-v-v-v-v, shzzzzzzz, v-v-v-v-v-v-v-v-v, shzzzzzzz.

I'll give you three guesses.

Wait. Let me do it for you again. Here. Listen.

V-v-v-v-v-v-v-v-v, shzzzzzzz, v-v-v-v-v-v-v-v-v, shzzzzzzz, v-v-v-v-v-v-v-v-v, shzzzzzzz, v-v-v-v-v-v-v-v-v, shzzzzzzz.

That's right. It's a breast pump as it sucks every last bit of life out of me through a series of suck-and-release moves, whereby my nipple is extended into a long plastic tube and then snapped back like a tired rubber band.

Now put little shake marks around the outside of the sound. You know the kind—like the little hash marks you used to put around the hips of those cartoons you drew of your fat fourth-grade teacher to make it look like her hips were shaking even when she stood still. That's right. Those. So put those little marks around the outside of v-v-v-v-v-v-v-v-v, shzzzzzzz, v-v-v-v-v-v-v-v, shzzzzzzz, v-v-v-v-v-v-v-v-v, shzzzzzzz, v-v-v-v-v-v-v-v-v, shzzzzzzz.

Good. Okay. Now—do you know what that is? It's a breast pump in the last stall on the right in the bathroom at work.

Here is where I pump while at the office: in the last stall on the right in the third floor bathroom. Note, I said third-floor, not tenth, which is where I actually work. I take my little red insulated bag full of ice-packs and bottles and pump to the elevator and travel down seven flights so as not to be making that noise in the stall next to the person that I may have to sit across from in a meeting in fifteen minutes or someone from whom I must demand an impossible deadline later in the day. I fear v-v-v-v-v, shzzzzz might lesson my leverage.

On three, I don't know a soul and nobody knows me. On three, I'm just an odd noise in the last stall on the right.

I have also pumped in the subbasement, a concrete tomb of wandering corridors off of which are tiny concrete rooms. I share one of these rooms with another department as storage for all my contest prizes. The subbasement is not ideal for pumping for a couple of reasons. First, I must take the freight elevator down and it is peopled with its own breed of citizen. I am fond of them but they can be a nosy crew and in a friendly sort of way, they like to know just where you're going, how long you're going to be there, and "Hey, nice bag, whattya doin'? Eatin' your lunch down der now?" Secondly, as I said, I share the room. So there I stand, breast bared, pump going strong, staring at the doorknob, and praying that my co-renters are not on their way down to pack up a few boxes or deliver a shipment of catalogs. And, thirdly, that same unique crew that peoples the elevator also roams the concrete corridors. I have this image of a long line of guys all wearing those very wide back-support leather belts around their waists, leaned up against my door looking to each other for a clue as to what that noise is.

My third option for pumping is Maggie's office on the occasion it is free of Maggie and available for my breasts. The problem with Scholastic is that is the land of open, free-wheeling idea exchange and creativity. That is to say that 95 percent of us are in cubicles and everyone else is in offices that are enclosed almost entirely with windows. Maggie has a rare office with only one window in the door and that window is *mostly* covered up by a poster of Britney Spears suggesting that kids should "Read It Baby, One More Time." But "mostly" when you're on the phone and "mostly" when you're bare-chested among coworkers are two very different kinds of "mostly covered." So I stack chairs in front of the gaps around the poster and hope that the v-v-v-v-v, shzzzzz doesn't create too much curiosity and resulting onlookers.

All in all, the third-floor stall is probably the best. Even there though, I take a deep breath when I hear the door open and close. My knee-jerk reaction is to quickly shut down the motor and stand perfectly still until I hear the door open and shut again with footsteps walking away. But that begins a nasty cycle because it's inevitable that someone else will come in before the first person has departed and before you know it you're standing there with this weird plastic contraption stuck silently to your left breast and you're trying to figure out which you heard, a door exit or a door entrance and just what was the count up to anyway? Are there three people in the bathroom now or four? And for Pete's sake! How long do they need to stand at the mirror? And then you decide, screw it, this is stupid. This is the ladies' room after all. All the participants at least have breasts even if they don't all milk them. But then kicking up the motor out of the blue is just too weird because all you can imagine is four heads turning to see where this sound is coming from when nobody has gone in or come out of a stall in minutes.

You just have to be strong and motor through.

That is what I was doing this morning when I heard a new sound.

Ready? Okay, what's this?

V-v-v-v-v-v-v-v-v-v-v-v.

Yup, that's a broken breast pump, one that got stuck in the

middle of a suck. It would have been better if it had broken in the middle of a release but the good news is, I was able to remove it from my person without too much trauma.

Replacement cost? One hundred and five dollars. And, therefore, I am presently opting to hand pump while Mom surfs the internet trying to find a contact at the manufacturer who will hopefully offer us a replacement free of charge as Callie really doesn't need to take on the cost of a second pump, considering all her other bills.

Hand pumping is not all bad. It's slightly more cumbersome but it's quiet.

July 10 — Tuesday

Callie is not paying for day care and that's huge. I can't even say how huge since I've had the luxury of not needing to care. But I know it's big. I should probably find out so I can hang it over her head if she ever talks trash about her gramma or questions my devotion or does anything at all that is, in any way, even the least bit unappealing.

Since the girl is not paying a red cent for day care, I support her in the gracious and generous move of fixing up Gramma's house with a goodly supply of baby-friendly items. Such as:

QTY/ITEM	CAT	PRICE	TOTAL
1 2-pk water chew toy	teething	1.29	
1 Shake n See rattle	boredom	1.79	
1 3-in-1 bouncy chair	furniture	25.00	

continued on next page

continued from previous page

1 Plush toy musical mobile	ambience	15.00	
2 4-pack Enfamil	grocery	15.98	
1 Baby nurser 4 oz.	dishware	1.59	
1 Benadryl	R&R	5.69	
1 NUK nipples	dishware	2.49	
1 Lead Check Swabs*	health & safety	7.20	
		$76.03	$4,691.23

*I actually purchased one of these myself very early on in the pregnancy and as a result had the entire barn repainted at a cost of $898 as it was thoroughly toxic. No bills for this maintenance have appeared on the child's register nor will they as I cannot put fifty years of wear and tear on her tab—toxic or not, the barn was going to have to be painted soon.

July 11 — Wednesday

Miss Bing of hand-me-down fame has celebrated her second birthday. As per our arrangement and in recognition of this event, Callie has sent along a lovely blue overall set.

QTY/ITEM	CAT	PRICE	TOTAL
1 Lovely blue overall set	gift	$32.20	$4,723.43

I would like it noted for the record that in our search for just the right outfit for Bing, we came across two outfits that were just right for Callie. With summer sales being what they are, we couldn't afford not to purchase them. And Lord knows, what the child really needs is another outfit.

Okay, perhaps that isn't exactly true. But these two items were really, really cute and I wanted to buy them because it fulfilled the deep materialistic hole in the center of my soul. Fine. I can acknowledge that. And so I'll comp them in recognition of my shallowness and unfulfilled self-realization. Please note that I am able to dissect my own pathological needs from my child's egoless, survival-based, pure, and sweet simplistic needs. I'm not entirely unhealthy.

Just for the record:

QTY/ITEM	CAT	PRICE	TOTAL
1 Yellow overall w/shoes	shallowness	$19.99 (comped)	
1 Really cute blue dress	unfulfilled self-realization	$23.80 (comped)	

While we were out, we picked up a few other items in the constant fight against nipple breakdown and gum flare-up. Someone told me recently that (and I can't imagine how this has been determined), if adults had to endure the pain of teething, we simply couldn't take it. Now, I appreciate the sentiment but really—I pushed this child out a hole that was nowhere near as large as her head. Is it possible I couldn't endure teething? Okay. I'll give the baby the benefit of the doubt and I will continue to purchase oddly shaped, water-filled, freezer-friendly suckie things until I find the one that finally works with hands that don't quite hit their target and a mouth that keeps opening and closing like a fish out of water. Life will get easier as the eye-hand coordination evolves.

QTY/ITEM	CAT	PRICE	TOTAL
1 Nuk NB nip	bottle maintenance	2.49	
1 Ansa teether rattle	gum maintenance	2.29	
1 J&J angled Muppet bottle	R&D	3.99	
		$8.77	$4,732.20

July 13 — Friday

Mom is the hero. She found someone awake and willing to pick up the phone at the breast-pump manufacturer. They have overnighted us a new motor and so I am ready to rise up to meet the work world again. It's unfortunate that upon my arrival to the third-floor bathroom this morning, I reached into my handy-dandy insulated pack and found that I had remembered the new motor and the backup hand-pump attachment just in case but had forgotten the cone-shaped breast attachment. I stood for a moment, staring into my bag and considered my options. I could get immediately on the next train back home; I could clutch my breasts all day and moan; or I could go purchase the cheapest possible hand pump I could find and muddle through the day. I opted for the latter and feel that billing the child for some degree of human error is acceptable.

QTY/ITEM	CAT	PRICE	TOTAL
1 Lansinoh exp hand pump	human error	$22.72	$4,754.92

July 15—Sunday

QTY/ITEM	CAT	PRICE	TOTAL
1 Offering	insurance	$5.00	$4,759.92

July 20—Friday

QTY/ITEM	CAT	PRICE	TOTAL
1 Aetna US Healthcare co-pay	insurance	15.29	
1 Vision @ $4.54	insurance	4.54	
		$19.83	$4,779.75

I am past due on a little accounting. It occurs to me that we are honing in on a few words I have not seen, used, or felt for some time. Routine. Regularity. Norm. Interestingly, it is the nature of my receipts that makes me think this. I stare at them and they stare back at me.

QTY/ITEM	CAT	PRICE	TOTAL
1 Pamper 15ct travel pack	travel/Chicago	1.89	
1 Pamper Bbyfr Wipes	sanitation	4.99	
1 Evenflo nurse pads	absorbtion	6.29	
2 4-pack Enfamil @7.99	groceries	15.98	
		$29.15	$4,808.90

We may be, as they say, what we eat, but I would suggest that equally, (if not more so), we are what we spend.

I am diapers and formula — I am wet wipes and breast pads. I am baby maintenance. I am Mom.

It's unnerving how quickly and completely that happened. I spent twenty years busting my hump to be a full-fledged writer and actor with no other distractions in my life. I wanted nothing more than to look back at a week and see no evidence of any other identity beyond writer and actor. Over the course of two decades, I don't believe I ever met my goal. I would wager a guess there was never a week when my receipts would have screamed out "actor and writer only!" There would have been signs of "waitress" (a receipt for Dr. Scholl's foot pads), "office manager" (five receipts from the same Korean deli salad bar), or "publicist" (one receipt for 672 postage stamps) in my wallet.

And yet, four months into this gig and there might as well be a neon sign flashing "MOM" on my wallet. It's as if I was never anything else.

I wouldn't mind seeing a receipt or two for actress (make-up) or a little writer Wite-out. Or, and I know this is just being silly — but imagine finding the stub of a movie ticket.

July 22 — Sunday

QTY/ITEM	CAT	PRICE	TOTAL
1 Offering	insurance	$5.00	$4,813.90

July 25 — Wednesday

Heat is the enemy of babies, at least my baby. I'll make a wild stab in the dark that she's not the only one. She hates it, makes her cranky as hell, turns her into Sally. And as much as I don't care for the choices Sally makes, I have to love her, have compassion for her. She's obviously a very close associate of dear Callie and therefore, I try to work with her.

It's not hard to understand, the crankiness. Think about it. You get four months under your belt and *bam-o!* you're hit with the dreaded triple H — hot, humid, and hazy. You get a little cranky 'cause there's no perspective. Can you imagine? You've just barely arrived and it's taken a little doing but you're feeling better — in fact, you're feeling pretty good about things. You've figured out that night vs. day thing and the fact that occasionally your mother's breast removes itself for her body and becomes a plastic cylinder that anyone can shove into your mouth. You've realized that diapers get wet but then with a little manhandling, they can get dry again. And though you don't quite understand why in the hell your mouth has to be on fire most of every day, you have worked out that sucking on all manner of flesh and fiber offers up a touch of relief.

So, you've got all that squared away and you're thinking it's just about time to kick back and enjoy a little down time when *whap!,* it's like a wall of wet diapers slapping you upside the head. Someone has fired up the ovens, cranked up the humidifier, and everyone around you seems to accept this earthbound hell without question.

And you think, so maybe this is what it is. Maybe the first four months was just part of the intro package. This is what the rest of life will be. It's never going to end. You're going to fry forever. There will never be another moment when you aren't sweating your ass off. It's only going to get worse from here.

Perspective. It's a valuable thing.

That's why we decided to go shopping today. Much money can be spent when the only goal is air-conditioning to relieve a sweaty baby from relentless howling.

Gramma went nuts. We hit every toy store in town and her house is now thoroughly babyfied.

QTY/ITEM	CAT	PRICE	TOTAL
1 Snappie bracelet	bday gift for friend	5.20	
1 Lamaze cloth cube	education/play	13.00	
1 Hotshot stuffed monkey	chew/play	3.20	
1 Rag doll	security/play	12.95	
1 Undershirt*	sleepwear	4.00	

continued on next page

continued from previous page			
1 Lamaze My First Mirror	reflection	20.00	
1 Activity pad	education/play	12.00	
		$70.35	$4,884.25

*This is a piece of clothing she actually needs, unlike every other piece of clothing she has ever received. She has outgrown all her other T-shirts and she truly needs a lightweight short T-shirt in this intoxifying heat because despite the fact that no shirt at all might be cooler in theory, in practice when one is being manhandled all day, skin on skin is too damn sticky.

July 31 — Tuesday

There are certain costs attached to saving money such as having to spend two airborne hours breast-feeding up against a severely pierced, very leathery, goatee-down-to-his-navel, Midwest cowboy who on some level thinks he's a member of ZZ Top.

We didn't have to. We could have bought ourselves out of this kind of situation. We could have bought Callie her own seat, secured a whole row. But we didn't, wanted to save the two hundred dollars. And therefore, Callie sat in my lap and I sat next to ZZ Top.

Of course, I saw him all the way at the other end of the plane as he boarded. I whispered, "Please God, not the goateed cowboy." But he steadily made his way back to the last aisle of the plane, looked at us, and said, "I think I'm in there," pointing at the window seat.

Goatee-man sat down. "How old?" he asked.

"Four-and-a-half months," I say.

"I've got an eight-month-old," he said and proceeded to show me not only pics of the infant but also of two other children. God bless America.

We are returned from Chicago, where Callie met her Gramma C, Uncle Dale, and Aunt Tommie. She danced and sang on cue and was very popular. She does know how to take a room.

From old friends on the paternal side, she also received more gifts. It's been a long while since the last accounting of gifts received and therefore, I believe it is time to update the list. Since last noted, she has received: five board books, a stuffed polar bear, a height chart, a photo album made from recycled paper, three antique fairy-tale books, one handmade sweater, a baby doll, a pant/shirt outfit, a pair of jelly shoes, three froggy bath mitts, sandals, a stacking toy, a crazy bird motion-clock, two autographed books, Beatrix Potter bookends, a linen dress, a pink velour outfit, a book on Greek myths, and a pewter mug.

As for the costs incurred on this trip to Chicago, it's time to settle up.

QTY/ITEM	CAT	PRICE	TOTAL
1 Airline ticket	family relations	192.50	
1 Avis Rent-A-Car	transportation	53.70	
1 Fuel refill	transportation	5.64	
1 Just for Me wipes refill	portable sanitation	2.39	
1 40-Pack Epson Photo Paper	memories	25.57	
		$279.80	$5,164.05

The flight home from Chicago was slightly less colorful than our ride there. Callie snagged her own seat though she still spent nearly the entire flight in my lap. She had a little snack at takeoff and then fell to a very sweet sleep nestled in my arms, leaning against her father. I stared down at her little face and battled off squeezing her so hard she'd wake up.

We slept together, the three of us, for the past two nights. All of us on the fold-out couch in the basement, it was the coziest of discomforts.

"She really loves it when all three of us are right together," I whispered to Lonnie.

He nodded. "So do I," he said.

August 3 — Friday

QTY/ITEM	CAT	PRICE	TOTAL
1 Aetna US Healthcare co-pay	insurance	15.29	
1 Vision @ $4.54	insurance	4.54	
		$19.83	$5,183.88

She's stealing time.

I keep thinking that if I overturn the right cushion or peek in the right nook, I'll find her stash — minutes, hours, days that she's just been yanking away from me and keeping for her own pleasure. Mom cried when she saw her after Chicago.

"She's older," she said.

And she was. Every day she is noticeably older like a time-lapse camera would show the growth—lengthening, widening, maturing. She pushes out from my grasp now so she can turn her little body forward and look straight at the world as she perches on my hip. That's a big-baby move.

And my hair is falling out. I know this is the result of hormonal shifts back from pregnancy and not because I am flashing forward into a bald old lady but nonetheless it makes me think there's time missing, disappeared with no clue.

For the record, this hair thing is bad. I have to roll down the window while I'm driving in order to let fly fistfulls of hair. Picture it. I'm driving along, running my hand over the top of my head and getting hunks of hair that I must send out into the speeding wind in order to untangle myself. This has been going on for weeks. I like my hair, consider it one of my identifying tributes. Callie will pay a hefty fee if this thinning doesn't curb itself soon.

I am on the 6:40 this morning, flying into the city for another day's work, the end of another week, the beginning of another month, the last of the summer and I'm seeing signs everywhere I look—time is not accounting for itself.

Clearly this is a not-very-masked fear of death.

Perhaps it was the dead bat in the bathroom this morning that has set me on this path. Five-forty-five in the morning and I stumble into the bathroom after feeding the girl and all but one step of my right foot away is a black mark on the rug. Breath stops. I stare, then make little hops backward, switch on the light. Bat, I think. Bat? In the bathroom? Dead? I wonder. Might be sleeping. I move quickly back into the hall, close the door swiftly but silently.

Touch Lonnie on the shoulder, his eyes slowly open.

"I think there's a dead bat in the bathroom," I whisper.

"Okay," he says, and moves naked across the room. I follow him.

"Maybe you could just wrap it in the rug," I say. "It's weird, right?"

"Yes," he says, "it's weird," and he moves himself out of the bathroom and down the stairs, bat going with him.

And I'm left to get dressed and slowly realize that of course it was Olga, our terminally kittenized cat, of course she somehow killed the bat and brought it upstairs to lay out on the rug.

Lonnie appears at the top of the stairs, batless and still only barely awake. He speaks softly, "Olga says she lured the bat in from the porch and it was so taken with her that it died of longing."

I look at him and smile.

"Good night," he says, kisses me, stumbles back to the bedroom.

And as I walked to the barn to get into the car, there was a mother deer and her little spotted baby walking out of the yard and across the street, like every day. And like every day, I tell the mama to be careful with her baby. There are fast cars down this road. And just down the road is my neighbor, who has been slowly dying all summer. When I saw his sister yesterday at the library, she said, "He's slipping away from us." He will be the second loss our small town will endure this summer, having lost old Warren Ferguson only weeks ago.

And the baby just keeps growing and changing and becoming, smiling and babbling all the way. Every day, she grabs something new and drops something old. I have always feared my own death most of all. Now there is something I fear more.

I will accept her time thievery—allow her to take my hours and my days as she pleases as long as she promises to never leave me. I want no time without her.

I offer all this up of my own free will. No charge.

August 4—Saturday

Before moving on to the business of the day—allow me to skeeve you out a bit.

After I'd gotten to work yesterday, I called Lonnie to suggest perhaps we should get the bat tested just to be absolutely sure, just in case someone got bit and we didn't know it.

Lonnie said he didn't know where the bat was. I asked him what that meant and he said, "It's not where I left it."

The bat wasn't dead. Wha! That makes my skin crawl.

QTY/ITEM	CAT	PRICE	TOTAL
1 Pampers Baby Fresh Wipes	sanitation	6.59	
2 4-pack Enfamil	groceries	12.78	
1 First Years bottle	dishware	2.19	
1 8-pack Gerber silicone nips	dishware	5.99	
1 6-pack Purell	sanitation	3.69	
		$31.24	$5,215.12

August 5 — Sunday

A small gift for my child — comped.

QTY/ITEM	CAT	PRICE	TOTAL
1 orchard short suit	style & grace	$18.00	(comped)

As opposed to these . . .

QTY/ITEM	CAT	PRICE	TOTAL
1 Pampers Stretch	sanitation	12.79	
3 4-pack Enfamil	bottled nutrition	9.87	
		$22.66	$5,237.78

Or this . . .

QTY/ITEM	CAT	PRICE	TOTAL
1 Offering	redemption	$3.00*	$5,240.78

* I forgot to go to the bank before church — my apologies to the various entities involved.

August 7 — Tuesday

Conversation with my agents, Number Two:

Very deep breath, dial.

"Commercials."

"Hi. Is Michael there?"

"Who's calling?"

"It's Betsy Howie. Returning his call."

"Okay. Just a minute."

Just a minute.

"He-e-e-e-e-y! How are you? We miss you!"

"I know. I'm sorry. I'm very guilty."

"Of what?"

"I've been avoiding you guys like the plague."

"Yeees?"

"Because I'm having a really tough time getting this weight off."

Exhale.

"Oh. Hey. Well, listen, I just wanted to see how you were really. We miss you and I just didn't know what was going on with you, if you were ready to come back, if your head's in it — regardless of the other . . ."

"Well, I do want to come back but it's true. I just don't know how . . . even if . . . when . . . I lose this weight . . . how I will do the running back and forth from the city. I'm already coming in two days a week and I just don't know if I can do more."

"Well — if you're up for it — we can send you out on the days you're in assuming if you get a call-back or a booking, you'll figure out a way to get in."

"Do you think it's a good idea for casting directors to see me like this?"

"Aaaah—that's a point. But the stuff you booked before—a lot of it—you could have been overweight."

"I'm going to get this weight off, I just don't know—"

"I know it's hard. We just had one of our clients come in—she had her baby a few months ago—she gained sixty-five pounds! She's basically got it off now."

"She's got it off already?! How old is she?"

"Ummm—forty—forty-uhhh-four."

Silence. (Well, almost silence—I might have been emitting a low growl.)

"I should preface that by saying she's a former Ford model."

"Yeah. You should."

"Well, just tell me what you wanna do."

"After Labor Day, I'll start going out on the two days that I'm in."

"Can I just ask you—how—well, how much?"

"Thirty."

Silence. (Imagine if I'd actually told him the truth?)

"Uh-huh."

"But it's spread out. I'm still in proportion, I just take up more space."

August 9 — Thursday

QTY/ITEM	CAT	PRICE	TOTAL
1 Jumbo Pampers Size 2	sanitation	28.59	
1 Jumbo One-Up Wipes	sanitation	10.99	
		$39.58	$5,280.36

August 13 — Monday

She will be five months old tomorrow and she is showing defi-
nite signs of aging. One thing is becoming perfectly clear — it's
expensive to mature.

Mom's been pointing that out continually since settling herself into retirement, with its medicare coverage, insurance supplements, and lack of prescription plans. But I see now that the
costs incurred due to aging do not begin at retirement.

Callie will soon acquire a significantly greater debt due simply to the fact that she has gained a relatively good hold on her
neck. That simple achievement makes her eligible for a brand-
new group of activities and the accompanying products that allow them — such as self-bouncing with the help of a door-frame
bouncy chair and upright dining in the comfort of her own
high chair.

But it's not just neck control. There is also the advancing digestive track that requires larger bottles, more formula, and
soon, even rice cereal. So, then of course, you also need spoons

and bowls and bibs. Then there are the ever-quickening hands that beg for more and more choke-free, nontoxic toys to grab and shove into the mouth. You can, of course, forego the expense of these little baubles but please know that you must then allow for the fact that you will most likely be entirely bald within the month as your child will cling mercilessly to your locks until you find some way to unlock that tiny Vulcan grip using a pair of pliers, a swift and sharp snip of the scissors, or some form of electric-shock therapy.

And, of course, there will be a good solid round of safety and security products that will be employed once she starts scooching around, which I must say, I expected by now. She rolled over for the first time at least a month ago but she really hasn't bothered to do it again. She didn't particularly enjoy it the first time and I am concerned that she has decided to remain on her back for the duration—live out her life like some kind of dyslexic turtle. It is assumed that the child is generally advanced and seriously gifted and therefore, she should be scooching by now.

I do hope the tally is not thwarting her. Perhaps she has caught wind of the escalating costs due to progress and has decided not to change. That's worrisome.

QTY/ITEM	CAT	PRICE	TOTAL
1 Spring water	food dilution	.67	
1 Gerber rice cereal	bulk	1.50	
1 Safety 1st spoons	bulk transportation	2.99	
1 Lenders mini-bagel	gum relief	2.89	

continued on next page

continued from previous page			
2 4-pack Enfamil	nutrition	12.98	
1 Ansa bottle	grippable nutrient transport	3.29	
1 Jump Up	upright activity	19.99	
		$44.31	$5,324.67

August 14 — Tuesday

There are mornings—and I guess this is one of them—when I have to admit to a slight sense of relief when I drive off at 5:55 A.M., headed for the train. My right arm hurts and I've got a kink in my neck and the whole of my body feels achy and tight. It will do me good to have this thirteen-hour break from carrying her. And from bouncing and rocking and swinging and walking and cajoling her away from screams, grumblings, and other expressions of discontent. Of course, I'll miss the smiles and belly laughs, too. But still—the break will be good.

Lonnie and I had an argument this weekend about a dinner invitation, which he was inclined to decline simply because there are not enough hours in the day and I can't disagree with him but there is creeping up on me this sense that we are losing ourselves in babyland.

Okay—maybe "we" aren't but I am.

There is a growing list of invitations I am simply declining because the logistics are too tough. Cool things too—Broadway openings and hot-shot concert tickets and weekends at the shore. It would be possible. I certainly have more help than the average Joe, but it's not easy or anxiety-free (read: guilt) and part of breezing into these sorts of events is to actually "breeze"—to be light and carefree. I am not convinced that one can ever breeze again, once one has given birth to a baby.

Movie stars—I suppose I've seen maternal movie stars breeze, but I suspect they are acting. Inside they are lugging their tired bodies along, drilling themselves on the details.

Are there enough bottles in the fridge? Will she scream at bedtime if I'm not there? If we leave here within an hour, as-suming standard traffic, can we make it back in time for her first middle-of-the-night waking?

I think maybe the movie stars think those things, too, and they are just pretending to breeze for the cameras. Or maybe not. They are movie stars, after all—it could be they just can't help breezing.

Once, I was pretty cool and relatively hip, with a date book that made for decent reading. I used to breeze. I would like to breeze again. Although it's hard to breeze at this weight; I sus-pect the effect might be more like a wind.

And of course, it's not that simple. In the midst of this relief, I already miss her and have already started calming the ever-roiling ball of anxiety that lives somewhere in the lower left-hand quadrant of my torso whenever I am on my own now. By 6:45 tonight, I will be screaming 'round mountain bends and slow moving traffic to get to her not a moment later than necessary.

Bottom line, there is no easy answer. Things are more com-plicated now. That's never clearer than when I'm getting ready to go away. This time, it's just me and Callie and we're headed to Michigan for a visit with Grandpa Dad, step-Gramma Wendy (still looking for a suitable baby-friendly title), and

Aunt Sarah. We don't leave until Friday and yet we started packing on Monday. So, there you have it—a four-day vacation takes four days of packing.

She is five months old today.

August 15 — Wednesday

QTY/ITEM	CAT	PRICE	TOTAL
2 Enfamil conc	groceries	6.58	
1 4-pack Enfamil	convenience	7.99	
1 Evenflo nurse pads	the final absorbtion?	6.29	
		$20.86	$5,345.53

August 16 — Thursday

Here is the significance of yesterday:

1. Mom had her first appointment with her new oncologist and:
   a. She is now 2½ years removed from her breast cancer diagnosis and everything appears to be okay.
   b. She liked the doctor.
   c. She didn't get lost getting to the appointment.
2. Mom noticed that the road to Sharon is "a beautiful drive."

After the doctor's appointment, she came over to the house to tell me about it. After a full report, she settled into a little seamstressing on one of Callie's outfits and I went to set up bottles for the next day.

Out of the quiet, Mom said, "Boy, that's a beautiful drive over there."

And I said entirely the wrong thing. I said, "Was it really completely unfamiliar?"

This response is born out of the fact that Mom doesn't acclimate all that quickly when it comes to navigation. Roads we've taken a dozen times draw a blank stare when I'm trying to give her directions. Sometimes, it makes me a little tense.

But I should have curbed my response because this morning, as I drove to the train through the endlessly gorgeous Berkshire Mountains, along the Housatonic River with the mist rising and the river bouncing over jagged mountain rocks and turkeys running and deer grazing and it is just so really truly stunning—it struck me how huge it is that Mom saw the beauty.

She was finally able to lift her head, take a breath, and look around. Up until now, she has been ruled by fear, driving scared, that whether by a little or by a whole state, she was in great danger of getting lost. This is my summation but I don't think I'm wrong. Up until yesterday, I suspect she was just too afraid to see anything but the very narrow "way."

Nearly every person I know has asked me in the last months, "How's your mom doing? Is she adjusting? Is she liking it?" I never know what to say. She's nuts for the baby and that's the mainstay. As for the rest, I'm not sure.

I asked her the other day.

"Well," she said. "I get depressed but I suspect I'd be getting depressed in Michigan, too. It's more a matter of getting used to not working than it is being here."

"You need a passion," I told her.

"I have a passion."

"Besides the baby, Mom."

"It's not just the baby. It's all of you."

"Something else—writing, gardening."

She did her eyebrows-raised, mouth-corners-turned-down, head-cocked thing that means, "Humph, well—that's somethin' to think about. But not now. Now, I will make you a snack."

Anyway, I have my answer. Next time I get the question, "How's your mom doing?" I'll say, "She's beginning to take in the scenery."

August 17—Friday

QTY/ITEM	CAT	PRICE	TOTAL
1 Aetna US Healthcare co-pay	insurance	15.29	
1 Vision @ $4.54	insurance	4.54	
		$19.83	$5,365.36

August 18 — Saturday

QTY/ITEM	CAT	PRICE	TOTAL
1 "Up North Michigan" sweatshirt	tourism	18.00	
1 Green wooden frog rolling toy	T&E	14.00	
		32.00	
		$32.00	$5,397.36

August 20 — Monday

I don't remember much — only an endless maniacal screaming as the plane taxied to the runway. And took off. And reached cruising altitude. And flew. And then landed. Squeezed into the middle seat between understanding men but nonetheless, men, who were so much closer than they ever wanted to be to a hysterical baby and her breast-feeding mother. And nothing worked and things dropped and I couldn't reach the diaper bag and there was turbulence so I couldn't get up and —

Oh, I can't go on. I cannot relive it.

I was the person other parents pitied and everyone else despised.

I think the baby has just succeeded in saving us the airfare of traveling to Minneapolis for the family wedding next month.

Here are the sweetest words I've ever heard: Flight attendants, prepare for landing.

Subj: Nice to have you visit
From: wendy@internet.com
To: Callie@dot.net

Thanks for coming to Michigan to see the BIG LAKE and the BIG DOG! Hope to see you next month, too.

Love and kisses and smiles to you and your Mom,
Wendy, Sarah, & Grandpa

Subj: Nice to have you visit
From: Callie@dot.net
To: wendy@internet.com

Thank you very much for letting me visit and taking me to the BIG LAKE with the BIG DOG who goes WOOWOOWOOWOOWOO-WOO and I liked that much better than the very terrible plane ride home that took seven hundred days so I was forced to scream like a maniac to maintain my baby pride because you cannot tolerate that kind of bad management without saying something or else the airlines might think it's okay to screw up everybody's day so I screamed like a maniac and everybody on the plane said wooooooooow, which is a little different from woowoowoowoowoo, but anyway I had a really really good time with you and Grandpa and Aunt Sarah and I will see you soon except that Mom says maybe not Minneapolis because there's no way to get there without connecting flights and she looked at me and said no way and I don't know what she meant but I can't worry about it right now because I have to go scream some more or I might get behind schedule and Mom says she's sending you pictures by snail mail so I guess she is because she always keeps her word.

Love,
Callie

August 21 — Tuesday

I'm trying very hard to prove to myself that life is only different in the best possible ways and that the old life with its travel
and adventure does not have to be dead and buried just because of a baby. With the right attitude and smart packing, the
fun and games can go on. That's what I say. But even a simple
weekend away demands a certain amount of recovery time. It's
making it harder and harder for me to believe myself.

Mom on the phone says to me as I'm sitting in the office the
day after our return, "It's been a high-maintenance day. She's
fine as long as you don't put her down—but Lord love a duck
if you put her down."

Lord love a duck? It must be bad. I've never heard my
mother talk like that.

August 22 — Wednesday

QTY/ITEM	CAT	PRICE	TOTAL
1 Travel boycott rebate*	credit	+ $875.00	($1,617.50)
*Canceled Minneapolis trip: 2 airline tickets, 2 nights in hotel, 1 weekend car rental			

August 24 — Friday

QTY/ITEM	CAT	PRICE	TOTAL
3 Enfamil Iron conc	groceries	8.97	
1 Gerber First Banana	groceries	.45	
1 Tylenol Infant	noise reduction	8.59	
1 Nuk nipples	grocery delivery	2.49	
		$20.50	$5,417.86

August 26 — Sunday

QTY/ITEM	CAT	PRICE	TOTAL
2 Gerber First Banana	groceries	.89	
1 Spring water	grocery dilution	.67	
		$1.56	$5,419.42

August 27 — Monday

I've been trying to buy a high chair for three days now. A lack of selection, the wrong selection, or no selection at all at a number of different stores has thwarted my efforts. I even tried to order the damn thing on-line, deciding on the most expensive one I could find just for kicks (I was only going to bill Callie for half). But it was out of stock.

I find this lack of purchasing power distressing. I am beginning to notice a trend. I am shopping a great deal these days. I have never been much of a shopper but I suspect I am doing it these days to mark moments in this strange kind of everchanging monotony that is the life of a wee child. I was really looking forward to bringing home that high chair.

I am pushing my baby along with the endless purchase of new equipment based on even the slightest sign of maturation. I am shuttling her through a stage that I, on the other hand, cling to. She is so sweet right now, so alive and fresh. I am certain I will look back at this time and realize that it was one of the finest of my life. To watch her as she figures out a new reach or a push off, it's heartbreaking and exhilarating, very rich and textured. It is the best of times and yet, I cannot wait to see her sit in a high chair and eat with a spoon.

This shifting monotony is strange. She is growing and changing every day and yet, every day her needs are much the same—all of me, all the time. To go to the store to buy a new rattle with a slightly higher level of functionality makes physical the changes that otherwise might be viewed as slight. They are not slight. She's growing like a maniac.

Someone told me recently that if we continued to grow at the rate that we do as babies, by the time we were thirty, we'd be bigger than the world.

I shouldn't need to shop with that kind of revolution going on in the living room. But I do. I want that high chair.

August 29 — Wednesday

QTY/ITEM	CAT	PRICE	TOTAL
1 Gingham Bugs stroller	Gramma transportation	14.99	
1 4 Stage feeding seat	Gramma dining	29.99	
1 Teething bib	Gramma cleanliness	4.99	
4 Enfamil Iron conc	nutrition	11.96	
1 Stack'm up cups	cognitive reasoning	3.79	
		$65.72	$5,485.14

August 30 — Thursday

I have agreed to my first crash-deadline writing job since Callie's birth. Scholastic loves to call me when they need a ninety-six-page manuscript written in a week. I used to do it all the time. It's stressful but the upside is that it's usually a little more lucrative and it's quick—obviously. You close your eyes, run like hell, and when you open them, you've got more money than you did. It was simply a matter of putting everything else second until the job was done

News flash. Callie doesn't cotton to being second. So yesterday, I did the only thing I could do. I strapped her on my front side by way of her Baby Bjorn and while she screeched and cooed and kicked everything off my desk, I pecked away at the keyboard, honing and rehoning the cliff-hanger that will be the spine-tingling chapter 4 ending of *Pokemon: Mewtwo Returns*.

August 31 — Friday

QTY/ITEM	CAT	PRICE	TOTAL
1 Aetna US Healthcare co-pay	insurance	15.29	
1 Vision @ $4.54	insurance	4.54	
		$19.83	$5,504.97

One of the high-rolling muckety-mucks at Scholastic stopped me in the hall.

"How is it, coming back to work?" she asked me.

"Fine," I told her. "Well, actually it's complicated."

"It never stops being complicated," she replied.

Brevity. It's a fine quality in a muckety-muck.

Evenflo Company
1801 Commerce Drive
Piqua, OH 45356
Attn: Customer Service

September 2

Re: Evenflo Easy Comfort High Chair, Woodland
    Design/Model #2851160A
    Manufactured on 6/13/01 — Purchased from Toys
    "R" Us, Kingston, NY — 9/1/01

Dear Sir or Madam:

I am writing in regard to the above-mentioned high chair.

I was so excited yesterday when I got in the car with my mother and five-month-old baby to drive an hour to the Toys "R" Us in Kingston, New York. We'd been planning all week to purchase the baby's new high chair as she is sitting up now and ready for this milestone.

I chose your Easy Comfort High Chair because it seemed to live up to its name — easy. Particularly appealing was the one-hand tray release. I was very impressed when I tried it in the store and it glided in and out of place with barely any effort.

When I returned home, I immediately unpacked the chair and screwed the snack tray in place. Then I unboxed the larger tray and slid it into place so that my husband could see the chair completely assembled. Now it was time to put the baby in the chair.

Perhaps you can imagine my disappointment when I depressed the one-hand tray release and found the large tray wouldn't budge. I struggled with the chair for fifteen minutes but could not get the tray to release. It moved slightly on the left side but the right side was absolutely stuck. I maneuvered the baby into the chair behind the large tray just so I could see what she looked like sitting in her new chair. But the moment was ruined. I realized I would probably spend the next day driving back to Kingston to return the chair.

After the baby went to sleep, I tried again to remove the tray. Lying on my back on the kitchen floor with my feet against the snack tray, I depressed the release button and pulled with all my might. Finally, the large tray came flying off the chair.

I trust this is not what you intended when you labeled this an "easy one-hand release."

I am desperate not to spend another two hours in my car in order to return the chair. The rest of the chair works beautifully. Can you possibly offer up some suggestions to make this tray function as it should? I hesitate to use any kind of oil because the chair is plastic but that is the sort of thing it seems to need.

My baby is ready to use her new chair. Your immediate reply would be appreciated.

Sincerely,
Betsy Howie

QTY/ITEM	CAT	PRICE	TOTAL
1 Evenflo Woodland high chair	furniture	$99.99	$5,604.96

And on a different note altogether:

QTY/ITEM	CAT	PRICE	TOTAL
1 Offering	pew space	$5.00	$5,609.96

September 3 — Monday

The thing about having purchased a less expensive high chair than the one I had intended to get on-line is that it left me with a bunch of extra money. So I spent it on new fall clothes for the girl.

We all know she does not need clothes but here's the emotional reality of the situation — I walk into baby-clothes stores now and most of the stuff that flips me out because it's so damn cute is now too damn small for Callie. I only just got warmed up on this baby-clothes thing and she's already out of it. Granted, there are still many cute things to buy once one grows beyond the twelve-month stage but there aren't *as* many and they aren't *as* cute. So, in the waning moments of her life as a twelve-month-size baby, I'm going to buy whatever the hell I want whenever I see it. I'm not having another baby. I won't ever get to do this again. Besides, things were on sale.

QTY/ITEM	CAT	PRICE	TOTAL
1 Blue flowered onesie	fall wardrobe	7.99	
1 Blue flowered pants	12-month size	3.49	
1 Pink striped onesie	long sleeves	7.99	

continued on next page

continued from previous page			
1 Pink pants	warmth	4.00	
1 Shirt-overall set	last hurrah	17.99	
		———	
		$41.46	$5,651.42

And or course, there are always the necessities . . .

QTY/ITEM	CAT	PRICE	TOTAL
1 2-pack Avent medium flow nipples	tableware	3.99	
1 Avent soft spout sippy cup	drinking	5.99	
		———	
		$9.98	$5,661.40

It's also worth noting that while we are at the Toys "R" Us, Callie pulled her first "Mommy, get me that!"

As I mulled over the selection of high chairs, I noticed an amazing group of toys on display above the high chairs. It was a collection of very impressive walkers and saucers. The saucer belongs to a family of toys wherein the child is slid into a seat positioned in the center of a doughnut-shaped tray. The tray has a dozen different kinds of toys affixed to it. The seat spins around on little casters allowing the child to travel in circles so that the full compliment of toys are fully accessible. It's basically the same concept as the old Horn and Hardart Automats, but in reverse—the food stands still and the people are on rotating shelves. Though, unlike Horn and Hardart, the entire contraption (in case the spinning and toys aren't enough) both rocks and bounces.

I pulled one off the shelf and put Callie in it. She squealed, grabbed the bouncing bumblebee, fought with me to chew on the water-filled flower, and punched at the musical worm. She looked like a really short CEO hard at work at her desk.

It couldn't have taken more than fifteen seconds. She flashed me this big kick-ass smile that for all intents and purposes said, "Mommy, get me this!"

But I was strong. I pulled her out of the toy, selected the high chair I meant to purchase, and headed home.

September 4 — Tuesday

Today, we drove to Waterbury and bought a saucer.

QTY/ITEM	CAT	PRICE	TOTAL
1 Evenflo Ultrasaucer	T&E	$84.79	$5,746.19

September 5 — Wednesday

QTY/ITEM	CAT	PRICE	TOTAL
6 Cans Enfamil	groceries	17.94	
2 Bananas	entertainment	.48	
		$18.42	$5,764.61

September 9 — Sunday

QTY/ITEM	CAT	PRICE	TOTAL
1 Offering	odds	$5.00	$5,769.61

September 10 — Monday

From my answering machine:

Hi, this call is for Betsy Howie. This is Colleen. I'm calling from Evenflo Company in Piqua, Ohio. We received your letter in regard to the Easy Comfort High Chair. If you'd like to give me a call back, we do have another tray and snack tray that we replace with the problem you're having with that high chair. So, please give me a call. I'll be happy to assist you. Thank you.

I have returned Colleen's phone call and they're sending me another set of trays. However, as I mentioned to Colleen, I'm not sure how I will employ a second snack tray as Lonnie and I, pulling together, were unable to detach the original one when we were trying to remove the large tray. Colleen said, "Yeah. You have to give it a good tug. It is supposed to be permanent once you put it in there but it will come out if you tug."

I was hoping for a free toy or something.

And thus, another fiscal quarter comes to an end. The baby will be six months old on Friday.

She can:

- Roll over (though she still doesn't like it)
- Hold up her head while on her belly
- Pick anything up and deposit it into her mouth
- Pet the cat
- Sit up (as long as an extra pair of hands are nearby)
- Screech like a wild animal
- Laugh deep belly laughs
- Clear her throat so as to make an opera diva's toes curl
- Stand up when held around the waist
- Eat bananas

She owes:

Credits: $1,617.50
Disbursements: $5,769.61

The Third
Fiscal Quarter

~

Deficit Spending

September 12 — Wednesday

The thing about having a baby is this: it clarifies the world for you or, that is, the worlds. There are two of them — the one "out there," with a general population that is prone to chaos and ugliness and the one "in here," with me and baby where minutia reigns and things run like clockwork — albeit a clock painted by Dali.

That means you can wake up to a morning of horror stories spilling out of the TV and still you put the bottle in the warmer and gurgle back to the baby as you change her diapers. Even when "out there" delivers up nightmares great enough to alter your perception of the world in which you were prepared to live with your baby, even then, you roll a ball across the floor and clap your hands when the baby reaches for it. You still do countless half-stooped laps in the living room with small hands clinging to you as small feet make tracks.

Living "in here" can be an unadulterated gift—priceless beyond compare, more than enough to clear any debt.

September 14—Friday

Callie is six months old today.

September 16—Sunday

QTY/ITEM	CAT	PRICE	TOTAL
1 Offering	help	$10.00 (comped)	

September 18—Tuesday

The monotony can make you nutty or it can keep you sane. For better, for worse, rain or shine, sleet, hail, or dark of night, the baby rumbles on like the U.S. postal system.

Whatever else is happening in the world, the baby still eats.

QTY/ITEM	CAT	PRICE	TOTAL
7 Cans Enfamil	nutrition	.93	
1 Spring Water	nutrition mixer	.75	
2 Bananas	eating practice	.50	
		$22.18	$5,791.79

The baby still makes a mess.

QTY/ITEM	CAT	PRICE	TOTAL
1 Shout Refill	laundry	4.99	
1 Spray 'n' Wash Stick	laundry	2.69	
		$7.68	$5,799.47

And the baby still needs protection.

QTY/ITEM	CAT	PRICE	TOTAL
1 Aetna US Healthcare co-pay	insurance	15.29	
1 Vision @ $4.54	insurance	4.54	
		$19.83	$5,819.30

September 19 — *Wednesday*

There is no fluoride in the water here in my little town. This is quite a shock. Dr. Brown explained the situation to me at Callie's six-month checkup today. Small towns, it seems, do not generally have fluoride in the water. It's too expensive. So, as if the three terribly painful shots weren't enough, he also prescribed fluoride drops. I must administer these drops to the child daily.

"For how long?" I asked.

"Until she's fourteen or sixteen."

I began to calculate the months into years and then I realized, he meant years. I was stunned. Sixteen years?

My mother has subsequently assured me that as Callie gets older, the dentist will offer a fluoride treatment that will replace this drop business. But nonetheless, I find it all very hard to believe. I had grown so confident in the decades since my childhood that fluoride flowed freely throughout this great country of ours.

But it's not true. It's just another false sense of security.

QTY/ITEM	CAT	PRICE	TOTAL
1 Fluoride drops	dental hygience	8.79	
1 Doctor co-pay	general upkeep	15.00	
		$23.79	$5,843.09

September 22 — Saturday

QTY/ITEM	CAT	PRICE	TOTAL
7 Cans Enfamil	nutrition	$20.93	$5,864.02

September 23 — Sunday

I have decided to no longer bill Callie for church offerings. I am not up to a full-scale spiritual scan in order to explain this shift in my thinking. It is what I have decided to do and that will have to suffice. Because I said so.

Don't get any funny ideas. I'm still only going to church to hold the baby and sit next to Mom since she has no desire to join the community aspect of the congregation with their post-sermon klatches whereupon she might find herself a Lutheran buddy or two. I'm afraid that kind of socializing makes Mom's skin crawl. She prefers her religion straight up, no frills — no coffee, no doughnuts, no chit-chat with fellow pewsters.

"Fine," I say every Sunday when she shakes her head to the notion of going downstairs for coffee. But I don't mean it. It's not fine. Not in my humble opinion. If you're going to spend the time singing the songs and reciting the words, isn't it just as important to show up and be counted as a coffee-drinking stand-up kind of Protestant willing to listen to your neighbor, willing to share a few recipes of your own?

But Mom and I have been battling this out for years. The

more significant question is why I thought moving 650 miles closer to an ocean might change her point of view.

So I get up on Sundays and put on black. I dress the baby in something fabulous and we toddle on down to the tiny one-room church so Mom won't be alone.

I know it's my problem, of my own making, but I had this fantasy when we first made plans for her to move out that she'd shake off the Midwest and dive into the life of our tiny town. I imagined her turning social like she's never ever been and laughing big on a regular basis. I had pictures of her snapping into a regular exercise regimen. I visualized her picking up one of the seven dozen blank books I've given her over the decades and finally returning to her writing.

I have dragged her into working the bid table at the auction for the library. I forced her to sell baked goods at the fair for the church. And I've made her sit through several brunches and lunches with neighbors and friends. She's hated all of it but she's done it because I wanted her to.

"If it's necessary, I don't mind," is what she says.

I just want her to reach out and make a friend, breathe deep, and take care of her body, find something that really excites her.

What I want for Mom is not unlike what I want for Callie.

I also want to win an Oscar—even though I no longer have an acting career.

September 24 — *Monday*

QTY/ITEM	CAT	PRICE	TOTAL
8 Enfamil	sustenance	23.92	
2 2-pack nipples	newer is better	6.98	
1 Pamper Premium	premium comfort	10.99	
		$41.89	$5,905.91

September 27 — *Thursday*

Who pays for Weight Watchers? Me? Or the kid?

I went to my first meeting last night. And as if simple attendance isn't humiliating enough, I ran into two of the women
from the animal clinic up the road. You really don't want to see
anyone you know at this kind of gathering. There's a real AA
feeling about it.

"Hi, I'm Betsy and I'm fat."

"Hi, Betsy."

Here's the deal. Rounding off numbers for the sake of convenience, I still have forty pounds to lose — okay, forty-five. I
haven't been totally honest about the full-blown damage of it
all. The truth is, by the time the baby was born, I was sixty
pounds heavier than I should be.

I will take responsibility for the first twenty as I was creeping up in that direction when I got pregnant. But the other
forty was/is absolutely, no doubt about it, ask me no questions,
I'll tell you no lies — Callie's. My daughter, who weighs in at 15

pounds 4 ounces and measures 26¾ inches, is in the 35th percentile for weight and the 75th percentile for height—she's the
one who gained this weight, not me. Can you imagine? Thirty-
fifth percentile for weight, seventy-fifth percentile for height—
she's the Kate Moss of babies. She's only six months old and
already I covet her figure.

I have lost fourteen pounds since her birth. Pathetic, I know,
but that's the fact. Until I lose the remaining twenty-six pounds
that will put me back where I started when she first came on the
scene, Callie will be picking up the weekly Weight Watcher fee.
After that, for the final twenty, I will take compete responsibility.

Speaking of figures—it's going to take me a while to wrap my
tired, estroged, estranged brain around this damn point system.

QTY/ITEM	CAT	PRICE	TOTAL
1 Weight Watchers weekly fee	reduction	$10.55	$5,916.46

By the way, here's a fun tip if you're bored some night—call
Weight Watchers' 800 number and Fergie will answer. She
says, "Hi. This is Fergie. Dutchess of York." She says "Hi," not
"Hello" and "How do you do." She's such an American.

September 28—Friday

Did you know that on the Weight Watchers plan, there are
three points in one eight-ounce serving of Enfamil formula?
Makes you think twice about having that second bottle.

QTY/ITEM	CAT	PRICE	TOTAL
1 Aetna US Healthcare co-pay	insurance	15.29	
1 Vision @ $4.54	insurance	4.54	
		$19.83	$5,936.29

September 30 — Sunday

She is 200 days old today.

October 1 — Monday

QTY/ITEM	CAT	PRICE	TOTAL
3 Enfamil	nutrition	$8.97	$5,945.26

October 2 — Tuesday

Home décor or baby care? Some items are very hard to categorize. My new area rug falls in the midst of that confusion. I
like the rug very much. It is earthy and yet has pretty pink
flowers. It will look very nice under the dining room table although it is not presently there. Because presently, it is living in
the living room, where it does not look all that swell but that's
fine. It's busy protecting Callie from the living room floor dur-

ing her daily calisthenics. She desperately needed a bigger area in which she could flail about in order to learn the difference between sitting up and falling over. Actually, she already knows that difference—the trick now is to figure out how one consciously opts for one over the other.

There are other moves too that she needs to develop, such as the "side lean into a forward support crawl position" as opposed to the "side lean into a face press against the floorboard position." And she could also use some work on the "belly flop to raised torso" move as well. Truth is, she's just not progressing all that quickly with any of the crawl-friendly physicalities.

I fear I am coddling her, carrying her too much, not letting her cry enough when she is doing that gasping-fish move on her belly. But I can't stand it when she's sucking up carpet fiber and screaming like it's the end of the world. Once it's degenerated to that point, she will refuse to execute the one move that I know for a fact she's already mastered—the rollover. She gets so pissed off at me for not rescuing her that she refuses to rescue herself. She's no dummy. She knows I can't stand watching her so unhappy and that when it finally comes, my rescue will be doubly fervent and affectionate to make up for her suffering. So she stays the course, committed to enduring that one last minute of face-press-fiber-sucking that'll turn the tide.

I've been contemplating how this behavior will look on a thirteen-year-old. I don't think it looks good.

She's paying for half the carpet.

QTY/ITEM	CAT	PRICE	TOTAL
1 5 x 8 area rug (½)	home decor/baby care	$184.97	$6,130.23

October 3 — Wednesday

QTY/ITEM	CAT	PRICE	TOTAL
1 Weight Watchers weekly fee	maternal reclamation	$10.55	$6,140.78

Down 3.6 pounds.

October 5 — Friday

QTY/ITEM	CAT	PRICE	TOTAL
7 Enfamil	cause	20.93	
1 Pampers Premium	effect	10.99	
		$31.92	$6,172.70

October 8 — Monday

I'm having trouble driving my car. I'm hitting a lot of things. So far this week, I have hit one deer, grazed another, and backed into my mother's car. My mother's car fared better than the deer — the first one that is; the second one just kept on running.

My car is the driving wounded — $1,500 worth of damage

and my deductible is $1,000. I wonder about the legalities of the insurance business.

I also wonder why I keep hitting things. Although, it's not a huge mystery—clearly I'm distracted. The question is—why? Is it because it's an insane world filled with insane people doing insane things that could drive the sanest person to distraction? Perhaps that's it, a simple matter of life and its challenges and their ability to distract. It's certainly plausible. If it proves out, Callie is free and clear, holds no financial responsibility.

But what if, in fact, this is the new me? This is me with a kid, forever and always.

Hi. How do you do? I'm distracted.

She takes up permanent brain space in a nonadjustable kind of way. What if I no longer have enough available RAM to drive fast while flipping through ideas, making notes, and working out problems? Perhaps those days are simply over.

Driving has always been important processing time for me. What if I no longer have the ability to do more than drive while I'm driving? Unless, of course, I wish to grow accustomed to hitting things—which I do not.

Do I charge her and if so, for what? The loss of brain time or the actual dent in the hood?

October 9 — Tuesday

I have my first audition today since more than a year ago. My agent called yesterday and I made the mistake of answering the phone instead of letting the machine take the call. He said he had an audition for me and I sputtered for a minute but was completely out of excuses. I said I'd go. So I'm going.

October 10 — Wednesday

QTY/ITEM	CAT	PRICE	TOTAL
1 Weight Watchers weekly fee	reduction	$10.55	$6,183.25

Down two pounds.

That means I got a little bookmark that says "I lost five pounds!" I put it on Callie's dresser when I got home. She is paying, after all. It seems only right she should own the ensuing perks.

October 11 — Thursday

I have a callback audition for that commercial — the audition from Tuesday. My first audition in a year and I get a callback and I couldn't be dreading the outcome more if I tried. I don't want this job. I don't want to figure out the logistics. I don't want to sneak away from Scholastic and then stroll back in as if I haven't been gone. I don't want to worry about my hair. I don't want to leave Callie for a long day of shooting tedious little pictures.

Of course, I wouldn't mind the money.

QTY/ITEM	CAT	PRICE	TOTAL
1 Aetna US Healthcare co-pay	insurance	15.29	
1 Vision @ $4.54	insurance	4.54	
		$19.83	$6203.08

October 12 — Friday

I went to the callback audition, waited forty-five minutes, calculated the potential income, and walked out. Couldn't justify the time.

October 13 — Saturday

QTY/ITEM	CAT	PRICE	TOTAL
12 Enfamil	rations-white	35.88	
2 Spring water	rations-clear	1.50	
1 Beechnut peas	rations-green	.50	
1 Beechnut peaches	rations-orange	.50	
1 Playtex Kindgrip Bottle 8 oz	more is more	4.59	
		$42.97	$6,246.05

October 14—Sunday

The child insisted on her own outfit while shopping today.

I was holding her in my arms as we circled the clothes racks and honestly, I was more focused on the clothes than I was on her. But then I felt a pull. We were snagged on something and unable to continue forward. I turned to see what was holding us up and Callie was looking at me with a clear sense of urgency.

She said, "Ah-ah-ah!" and her hand clamped on the sleeve of an outfit.

It's still the beginning of the beginning and yet it's the beginning of the end. She has developed her own sense of style.

Unfortunately—I'm just going to say it—her taste appears to be on the tacky side. The ensemble of choice is a pantsuit. The pant material is light blue polyester with a heart-and-chick pattern stamped on in a cheap pink and lousy green. The top is also light blue but it has a higher percentage of cotton in its blend, which means the blues don't really match since different materials take dye differently, I guess. Whatever. All I know is they don't look right together and she doesn't seem to care. Along the bottom of the shirt is a series of embroidered hearts and chicks in the same shallow pink and sickly lime green. I wouldn't be caught dead in such an outfit but then again, I understand that Callie is not expecting me to wear it.

I was not alone in my opinion. Mom didn't like it either. We tried to dissuade the baby but every time I offered up another option, she stared at it with cold eyes and then she turned those eyes on me.

Her opinion was clear—"Not in a million years!"

So I held up the tacky blue, pink, and green mess again.
She kicked and said, "Ah-ah-ah."

If there were only ever going to be one item on the tally, I
think this would have to be it. She is absolutely responsible.

I guess it's worth noting that her selection was marked
down to half price.

QTY/ITEM	CAT	PRICE	TOTAL
1 two-piece clothing disaster	personal freedom	$11.49	$6,257.54

Mom and I purchased a few other items—warm bits for
winter—more in keeping with the child's best fashion interest.

QTY/ITEM	CAT	PRICE	TOTAL
1 Inf, girl shirt	inflicted style	5.98	
1 Inf, girl pants	fashion bondage	5.98	
1 Floral longjohns	enforced materialism	9.99	
1 Green sleeper	enslaved model	9.99	
1 Rose stretchie	continued assault	10.00	
1 Miss Bunny sleeper	more of the same	10.00	
		$51.94	$6,309.48

A word on these purchases—the tide has shifted, the winds
of change have blown. Callie has grown and she doesn't have
nearly as many clothes as she once did. The laundry room is

overflowing with hand-me-down wannabes. We just need the "me" "down" to whom we will "hand" and they will move from wannabes to actuallies.

We're waiting to hear whether Carol is pregnant with a girl or a boy. If it's a girl, she's the big winner. She receives three sizeable boxes of Callie toss-offs. If it's not a girl, we'll weed out the androgynous items, send that stuff to Carol, and then the really girly stuff will go to Gale, assuming Gale's baby is a girl. (By the way, that's Gale of "my biological clock is digital." Guess even digital clocks go off eventually.) Anyway, if Gale's baby is a boy we'll wait to see if Laura's baby is a girl—there are a lot of pregnant people these days.

This first shipment will definitely be the mother lode. It's become quite clear that in order to keep Callie in the style to which she has become accustomed, I will have to drop a lot of dough and shop regularly. Neither is likely. The child dressed very well in her first six months and if it had been her desire to continue doing so, she should have thought about it before she grew.

October 15 — Monday

I have finally signed my will. Callie was there, sitting on the big lawyer conference table.

She laughed as the ink dried. I have opted to look past the behavior.

October 16 — Tuesday

A new collection of gifts have assembled—a Lamaze Peek-a-Ball play toy, a Lamaze Soft Sorter play toy, one red fleece coverall with hood, one used but in-good-condition booster seat, an "I Love NYC" T-shirt, a pumpkin Halloween costume, and one pair of beaded shoes with cat-head design.

Thank-you notes are underway.

QTY/ITEM	CAT	PRICE	TOTAL
5 Postage @.34	continued grace	$1.70	$6,311.18

October 17 — Wednesday

Mom says she didn't see the car behind the bus.

She says it was absolutely her fault.

I cannot say as I was in New York, at the office, running to meetings, cranking out copy, reading through thousands of contest entries. In general, enjoying my day off—which is absolutely what my days in the office have become.

At any rate, whatever happened, the fortunate end is that no one was hurt and the senior center is continuing on with its programs unaffected.

Mom, however, has gone through a notable transition. She is no longer the mysterious new neighbor. Everyone in town knows she is the lesser-senior who swiped the senior-er as the senior-er tried to pull into the parking lot of the senior center behind Town Hall.

You must understand that there's little else to our town beyond Main Street. We have a Railroad Street and a Prospect Street but really, "town" is Main Street. And Mom chose to have her little run-in on Main Street directly in front of Main Street's central location — Town Hall.

As luck would have it, while Mary Palmer, the town clerk, was out front waiting with Mom and Mrs. Violet Winthrop — the senior-er — for the State Trooper to show up, Cookie, the librarian, was coming out of Denny's garage. As a result, by the time Lonnie walked through the doors of the library on the other end of Main Street where Callie was supposed to be in attendance at story hour in order to inform Erica, the children's librarian, that Callie would not in fact be in attendance — Erica already knew.

Before Lonnie could finish saying, "I'm afraid we won't be able to make it." Erica leaned in and quietly said, "I heard."

Mom is still mystified as to how the whole ordeal came to pass. "I just don't know how you could run into anyone in a town this small," she said.

I know she feels rotten about Mrs. Winthrop but there's something else going on as well. I can't quite nail it but I swear there's the tiniest of grins on Mom's face, like she's a little bit tickled at the nature of life. She's more connected to our town and the people now. She's more likely to give a wave and nod as she passes Town Hall. Perhaps she didn't reach out and make a friend but her Honda did.

"I'm just amazed at how kind everyone was to me," she said for the third time, "especially Mrs. Winthrop."

"The next time you run into her," I responded, "you should invite her to dinner."

Mom laughed big.

October 18 — Thursday

QTY/ITEM	CAT	PRICE	TOTAL
1 Weight Watchers weekly fee	expensive hunger	$10.55	$6,321.73

Down 1.2 pounds.

I suspect Callie may one day argue this expense. I don't want to make it too easy for her but it occurs to me as well that most people who are really good at being hungry do it for free. So, in essence, she is paying for my lack of experience and training.

However, right now, she mostly says da-da-da-da-da, and I do not find that to be a compelling argument. The expense will stand.

October 20 — Saturday

QTY/ITEM	CAT	PRICE	TOTAL
10 Cans Enfamil	breast replacement	36.90	
1 Pampers size 2	toilet replacement	12.99	
1 Beechnut pears	toy replacement	.55	
1 Beechnut carrots	pear replacement	.55	
		$50.99	$6,372.72

October 21 — Sunday

Historical perspective is so important in times like these. Therefore, I submit the following comparison (thanks to the recent unearthing of my own baby book) in the name of education and understanding and because I find it just so darn alarming. A note for clarity: The bill that follows has not appeared on the tally as it has been paid through various insurances and flexcare programs. However, the historical relevance remains.

I spent two nights in the hospital when I gave birth to Callie. Here are the full charges for that stay:

Birth of Callie		
OB/2 Bed	2,253.00	
IV solutions	517.20	
Drugs/other	9.20	(I remember the drugs. I don't recall the other.)
Med-Sur supplies	387.05	
Laboratory	9.00	
Lab/immunology	40.00	
Lab/hematology	49.05	
Drugs/detail code	29.40	
Delivery room/labor	1,284.85	(Why was I charged for labor? Seems like if anyone's gonna get paid for that, it oughta be me.)
TOTAL:	$4,578.75	

My mother contracted spinal meningitis as a result of the epidural she received while giving birth to me. As a result, she spent almost two weeks in the hospital. Here are the full charges for that stay:

Birth of Betsy	
13 days @ $22.00/day	286.00
Operating or Delivery Room	30.00
Anesthesia	22.00
Laboratory	156.50
Drugs and dressings	213.10
Baby care (13 days)	156.00
TOTAL:	**$863.60**

So, a bed used to be $22.00 per night. Now, it's $1,126.50. That's 51 times more expensive.

Mom and Lonnie didn't seem to share my dismay. Mom said, "Well, chicken used to be twenty-six cents per pound." And Lonnie said, "I always figure these things out according to Hellmann's mayonnaise. I paid fifty-three cents a jar back then. Now it's three something."

Okay. So, then, chicken should be $13.26 a pound today and a jar of Hellmann's mayonnaise should be $27.03.

Perhaps there is more to be said for having babies when you're really, really young than I would have originally thought. Clearly, the sooner you have them, the cheaper they'll be. So that's my advice: Have your babies while you can still afford the mayonnaise.

October 22 — Monday

I have not yet alerted my agent to the fact that I no longer intend to go out on auditions. As a result, when the phone rang yesterday, I had to agree to go out again today. It was another mess. It was a "mom" spot.

I arrived to find about 612 children waiting for their chance to stare appealingly into the camera and suck down a slice of Kraft Cheese (served to them by a vapid mother with a warm smile).

This kind of audition is everything vile we already know — plus about 40 percent more grief because you have to 1. deal with the child, 2. be matched with a child that could plausibly be considered yours and so if that child is late, you wait — or risk being disqualified out-of-hand for appearing on-camera with a child who doesn't match, 3. you have to deal with the mother of the child, and 4. you have to sit in a waiting room (a.k.a. hallway) with all your competition, all the children, all the real mothers, and seven folding chairs.

It's good sport to run along the faces and do a quick count of the moms — real mom, auditioning mom, real mom, real mom, auditioning mom, and so on. It's not hard to figure it out. The auditioning mothers are not authentic. They look rested, coiffed, and thin. They look the way America wants them to.

I must say, I have always been amazed at the beauty of certain children when measured up against their gene pools as becomes apparent through their parent. It doesn't seem possible that the ringletted angelic being who knows just the right way to hold an individually packaged slice of cheese could have been spawned by the mother squatted on the folding chair at the end of the hallway in the stained orange parka drinking a coke and fondling the cigarette she'll be inhaling on the other side of this audition. But it's true, I guess. They can't all be adopted.

It's amusing that so much hoopla is made over which child goes with which "mother" because obviously anything can come from anything. But that's the way it's done. The child sits with its genetic mother until its name is called and then it is matched up with its physically attractive alternative.

Today as I fought my way through the masses in order to hold my place in line, I was mis-identified.

"Are there anymore three-fifteen moms?" screeched the stressed-out casting director.

"Yes!" I shouted. "I am a three-fifteen mom and I've been waiting for a half hour!"

Stressed-out casting director took one look at me and said, "No, not real moms."

Oh. It was a chilly moment.

It is perfectly clear. I am in no shape to be doing this. Somewhere in the last several months, I went and got authentic. I suspect that, at present, Callie is too attractive to be considered my daughter.

October 23 — Tuesday

Dear Michael:
   I know I've only gone out on a couple of auditions since we spoke on the phone and agreed that I would go

out on the days I was in the city, but it's become apparent in just those few times that I am not in a position to be auditioning right now.

I have gone round and round in my head about this because I don't want to lose my connection with you and the agency but my schedule is so tight currently that commercials just don't make sense. I am working a bare minimum number of hours at my "day job" so ducking out for an audition becomes a much bigger deal than it used to be. And this early time with the baby is (as everyone says) so fleeting that I'm trying very hard not to give up any more time with her than I absolutely have to.

Anyway, all this to say — I hope you will understand and that in a year or so when the baby's older and I'm in town more frequently, I will still be able to work with you. My fingers are crossed that my current situation won't sever the bond between me and you and the agency.

Betsy

October 24 — Wednesday

QTY/ITEM	CAT	PRICE	TOTAL
1 Weight Watchers weekly fee	unrequited hunger	$10.55	$6,383.27

Up .2 pounds. I don't like it. I don't understand it. I don't want to discuss it.

Before the weigh-in—back when I still thought I was having a good day—Callie and Mom and I went shopping for a birthday present for soon to be one-year-old Julie of Tokyo. I would purchase Julie a gift whether Callie was involved or not so Callie will not be billed for this item.

However, if Callie were not involved, I would not have picked up a second outfit while I was there, which I did. And which will be very cute on the girl.

QTY/ITEM	CAT	PRICE	TOTAL
1 three-piece suit	fashion maintenance	$34.00	$6,417.27

October 25 — Thursday

Daddy's birthday.

QTY/ITEM	CAT	PRICE	TOTAL
1 Speakerphone/ answering mach.	upgrading pop	$62.99	$6,480.26

On a completely different subject, Carol is having a boy. There is no big hand-me-down winner. The pot continues to grow.

October 26 — Friday

QTY/ITEM	CAT	PRICE	TOTAL
1 Aetna US Healthcare co-pay	insurance	15.29	
1 Vision @ $4.54	insurance	4.54	
		$19.83	$6,500.09

It's appropriate that Callie should make payment on her health-care policy today since there is enough snot in her head to choke a horse. My poor baby is so stuffed up that it's getting hard for her to take a bottle.

This has spurred me to get more formula in the house. Since she's not eating as much as I would like her to, my solution is to buy more for her to eat.

You don't sleep a lot when your baby is sick. Without sleep, the brain functions at a significantly lower level. I am evidence.

QTY/ITEM	CAT	PRICE	TOTAL
10 Cans Enfamil	medical remedy	29.99	
2 Organic baby food	only the best for my . . .	1.09	
1 8 oz Gerber bottle	remedy delivery	1.69	
1 Pediacare drops	another remedy	5.49	
		$38.26	$6,538.35

October 27 — Saturday

She is much worse. Today she is coughing, too. The Pedi-acare I bought yesterday only handles stuffy noses. We need full strength.

QTY/ITEM	CAT	PRICE	TOTAL
1 Pediacare drops	full remedy	$5.29	$6543.64

For the record, she has given up on the notion of sleep.

October 28 — Sunday

Daddy didn't like the ringer on his birthday present phone.

QTY/ITEM	CAT	PRICE	TOTAL
1 Speakerphone/ answering mach.	CREDIT	$62.99	($1,680.49)

Callie and I went for a ride to return the machine. It was my last hope at getting her to sleep. It worked — at least for a little while.

She's drooling like a maniac now, too. This may all be related to teething. It's time already for her to break through with some enamel. I'm certainly ready to be done with this little episode and if it takes having a tooth pop through, then so be it.

I believe there is room for me to argue an insurance claim here. As you will recall, I signed Callie up for dental from the very beginning and then in deference to my own OCD decided not to bill her for the coverage—at least not until she has teeth.

But since she does have the coverage and I am paying for it, it seems as though I should be able to file a claim for the pain and suffering (mine) in anticipation of the teeth (hers).

October 29—Monday

Otitis media—that's the diagnosis on Callie's doctor bill.

It's an ear infection. That means the baby has to start on her first round of antibiotics. The doctor saying this to me is Dr. Gray, not Dr. Brown, because during this first medical crisis, Dr. Brown is in Tokyo singing with his choir.

As we were wrapping up the appointment, I muttered, "So much for breast-feeding," and Dr. Gray said, "but you said you were weaning her."

"I am but I guess I thought the benefits of breast-feeding were more far-reaching," I told her.

I can't really tell you what she said in response to that—something about fluid in the eustachian tubes and swift sparkling river waters as compared to stagnant mucky swamp water. I don't really know because I was too busy trying to determine if the sudden cool chill I felt from the doctor when I informed her that I was weaning Callie was actual or due to my own guilt-ridden neurosis.

A real mother—a good mother—would have stayed with the breast-feeding for at least a year. I cut the babe off and what happens? She gets her first infection, her first antibiotic.

I checked in with Mom on this moment once we were in the car on the way to the pharmacy. She said that was hooey. She said she didn't sense any such thing from the doctor. When we got to the pharmacy, she wandered off in search of balloons to hang on her front door so the kids in the neighborhood will stop at her house on Halloween. She's afraid without the balloons to identify her, the kids might decide she's the crazy old lady in the haunted house.

Hooey.

So maybe the doctor judged me harshly and maybe she didn't, but I still feel bad. Callie is supposed to be a pumpkin on Wednesday and it looks like the Halloween parade is out of the question.

QTY/ITEM	CAT	PRICE	TOTAL
1 Bottle Amoxycillin	ear infection	3.60	
1 Doctor co-pay	insult to injury	15.00	
		$18.60	$6,562.24

October 30 — Tuesday

The will bill—it has arrived.

QTY/ITEM	CAT	PRICE	TOTAL
1 Will	legal and binding	$250.00	$6,812.24

October 31 — Wednesday

QTY/ITEM	CAT	PRICE	TOTAL
1 Weight Watchers weekly fee	shrinkage	$10.55	$6,822.79

Down four pounds! I would have received my "I lost ten pounds" sticker which is to be adhered to Callie's "I lost five pounds" bookmark, but I couldn't stay for the meeting. Lonnie was in the city and I alone was responsible for doling out the Halloween treats. The leader said they'd clap for me next week. I told her that would be just fine.

Four pounds. Perhaps I may, actually, one day, catch a glimpse of my former self.

I left the weigh-in feeling pretty great. But it didn't last. There's only so much glee you can feel when you're sitting alongside a pumpkin with a runny nose.

November 3 — Saturday

QTY/ITEM	CAT	PRICE	TOTAL
1 Pampers Mega size 2	bulk absorbtion	19.49	
1 Tender Harvest Banana	organic nutrition	.55	
1 Tylenol Baby Drops	misery avoidance	5.49	
10 Enfamil	canned growth	29.90	
		$55.43	$6,878.22

November 6 — Tuesday

Election Day. Lonnie and I took the baby in the stroller down to Town Hall to cast our ballots. As we approached the steps of the hall, Lonnie picked up the front end of the stroller and I lifted the back. Callie lounged comfortably throughout the flight.

As we lugged her up the stairs, a voice rang out from the street curb. There stood one of the dapper gents from the library board of directors. He was watching us.

"You can bill her for that too, you know," he shouted when we set the stroller down.

Obviously the word is out. Folks in town are talking.

"There she goes . . . she's the one who charges her kid for everything."

November 7 — Wednesday

QTY/ITEM	CAT	PRICE	TOTAL
1 Weight Watchers weekly fee	gradual disappearance	$10.55	$6,888.77

I'm up .4 pounds but I do not worry as I am in the midst of returning to a cycle that includes swelling up and deflating on a monthly basis. Presently, I am mid-swell. However, now that I understand the true meaning of the world "swell" as it relates to the female body, I am less likely to beef about this monthly business.

I remember thinking (back in my pre-pregnant days) that one of the things that would be great about being pregnant was that you didn't have to deal with a period for at least a year. Now, I will acknowledge that I did not have the most physically joyful of pregnancies and many women may disagree with me, but my post-delivery opinion is that I'd take the monthly bloat over pregnancy any day. Compared to forty weeks of puking, burping, pimpled expansion, the thought of a few cramps and a little retention rides easy. And I only have to wait a week for the tide to go out. It's a deal.

Everybody! Sing along if you care to—"I enjoy being a girl!"

November 8 — Thursday

QTY/ITEM	CAT	PRICE	TOTAL
1 Outrageously great dress	holiday fashion	56.00 (Comped)	
1 Pair perfect shoes for above dress	giving thanks footwear	32.00 (Comped)	

I have purchased an all-silk dry-clean-only dress for my almost eight-month-old daughter, which she will wear to the Thanksgiving banquet and steal the entire show. I have also obtained the perfect black leather shoes with tiny floral accents to accessorize said dress.

Of course, it's absolutely criminal to buy anything for a baby that's dry-clean only, much less a dress with crinoline. But there are times for criminals and this is one of them. She will look stunning in this dress and it will make me happy to see her in it. However, please note, I'm not deluded enough to think that the mere spending of $80 to dress my daughter like a princess is enough to consider me a good mother. In fact, I am aware that some might suggest I am being just the teensiest bit shallow to care.

I am untouched by such sentiments.

Once I walked into that fancy-ass store in Grand Central Station—where they are smart enough to open by eight in the morning so you can spend all your money before you're rational—it was a given that the child would be getting a gown.

The bottom line is this: I am comping Callie the dress and

shoes. It's the holidays and I want her to look nice. I'm allowed to pay for that.

After all, I am her mother.

November 9 — Friday

QTY/ITEM	CAT	PRICE	TOTAL
1 Aetna US Healthcare co-pay	insurance	15.29	
1 Vision @ $4.54	insurance	4.54	
		$19.83	$6,908.60

November 10 — Saturday

Common cold to earache to amoxycillin to unbelievable diarrhea to wicked diaper rash to major run on bum ointment.

QTY/ITEM	CAT	PRICE	TOTAL
1 Tube A&D ointment	chain reaction	4.49	
10 Cans Enfamil	key to chain	29.90	
		$34.39	$6,942.99

November 12 — Monday

QTY/ITEM	CAT	PRICE	TOTAL
1 Pediacare Drops	continued phlegm	$5.79	6,948.78

I am ill. I have caught the plague.

I cannot speak.

But Tory just called to say that if I wanted to get some quick pics of Callie in her Thanksgiving dress, she would be set up for two different shoots today and could squeeze us in between them.

We must go. This dress and this child — the team — must be recorded for the sake of history. Callie gets by without talking. I'm sure I can, too. I will wear a chalkboard around my neck should the need arise to communicate.

November 13 — Tuesday

I rise up from my DayQuil, NyQuil, WhatTimeIsItAnyway? Quil fog. I wave a white flag. Okay. Yes. It is a diaper. But who cares? I surrender. Cut me some slack. I can't take much more. I need sleep. I need air. How can I recover when the baby keeps up with her unrelenting schedule?

This must be bioterrorism. If it's not, then someone has definitely missed the boat. If the international array of "folks" looking to take out all Western thought really want to get serious about this annihilation business then they ought to consider the business of baby bioterrorism. They ought to be bottling baby snot. Crop dusters? Anthrax? Gimme a break. Snot from an international array of babies could, without question, destroy us all. We can't even handle our own genetically matched snot. Imagine what would happen if we all got slimed with the snot of faraway lands?

Gather it up—from Turkey, Bolivia, Canada, Monserrat, every nation, every nostril. Then, swap it around. Spray America with the Turk snot, England with the Bolivian snot, Germany with the snot of Iran and Japan. Douse China with Costa Rica, smear Russia with Greece, wipe Tibet with the Swedes. The possibilities are endless and devastating.

I have only the smallest of voices today. However, that is more voice than I have had in three days. I have never completely lost my voice before, not once in my life. I make my living from talking. I have no actual skills. I talk my way in and out of all forms of employment. Without my voice, I am unmarketable. This is billable and it's expensive. I now understand that I have never before had a cold. I bow to the baby and beg for mercy. She is eight months old today. She is a force with which to be reckoned.

QTY/ITEM	CAT	PRICE	TOTAL
1 Doctor co-pay	baby . . . not mother	$15.00	$6,963.78

November 14 — Wednesday

QTY/ITEM	CAT	PRICE	TOTAL
1 Weight Watchers weekly fee	downsizing	$10.55	$6,974.33

Down 1.4 pounds.

November 18 — Sunday

I was one of those people this afternoon. One of those people with a baby in the seat of the grocery cart, a list in my hand, and a cart so full and overflowing that the baby had to hold three cans of tuna fish in her lap. I was one of those mothers who stood in line and unloaded the cart with one hand, kept the baby from grabbing six packs of Juicy Fruit with the other hand, and tried to read as much of the *National Enquirer* as I possibly could without actually touching it.

I was a Mom getting ready for a holiday while keeping the shelves stocked with my family's everyday needs at the same time.

Now that may sound quaint and I suppose it is but I've had enough. This isn't funny anymore. I want to know who took my life. I want to know how he/she got it and I want to know where he/she put it. I want answers and I want them now because . . . because I just do. It's my life and I have a right to know where it is. I'm particularly curious if someone else is leading it right now because I find I keep seeing people who look very familiar in a haunting kind of way as I walk the streets of New York. I recognize something but I just can't place it. I think it's possible that I've passed my life on the street and just didn't know it.

It's not that I dislike this life I'm leading. It's particularly pleasant when the baby laughs at absolutely everything I think, say, and do. But that's beside the point. Someone has made off with my life and that's just not right. I want it returned. If nothing else, I would like to have it so I could take it out and look at it every now and then.

November 19 — Monday

For the holiday, the baby will not be picking up anything above and beyond her usual expenses. I'm covering the cost of the amazing frock and she's not being billed for a single ounce of the turkey.

So there you have it — I'm not completely without generosity.

QTY/ITEM	CAT	PRICE	TOTAL
1 Pamper Premium	same ol'	13.49	
10 Enfamil	more of the same ol'	29.90	
2 Gerber Nurser, 8 oz.	increased intake delivery system	3.38	
2 Gerber First squash	Thanksgiving for babies	.89	
1 Baby bananas	desserts for babies	.96	
		$48.62	$7,022.95

November 21 — Wednesday

QTY/ITEM	CAT	PRICE	TOTAL
1 Aetna US Healthcare co-pay	insurance	15.29	
1 Vision @ $4.54	insurance	4.54	
		$19.83	$7,092.78

QTY/ITEM	CAT	PRICE	TOTAL
1 Weight Watchers weekly fee	self flagellation	$10.55	$7,053.33

Up .2. This is getting old. Or is it me?

November 24 — Friday

Our first Thanksgiving has come and gone. The turkey was fine but more important, the dress made its first social appearance. Aside from the fact that Callie couldn't nap because the crinoline kept waking her up, the dress was a smash hit.

Callie was completely happy to stay in it all day long. Furthermore, she didn't get a single spot on it. She did pull one of her Ninja spit-up maneuvers—silent as the night—just leaned out over my arm and the next time I looked down there was a white abstract painting on the floor. But she didn't get the slightest splash on the silk.

Clearly, this girl was born for dry-clean only.

She was also born for complicated familial dancing, careful maneuvers that will allow all things for all people at all holidays. This year, Callie is spending this first holiday weekend with her maternal grandparents. Gramma was at Thanksgiving dinner along with ten of the babe's closest friends and then forty-five minutes after the dinner guests departed and Lonnie and I were still scraping potatoes off the china, Grandpa, Wendy, and Aunt Sarah arrived from Michigan to spend the rest of the weekend. Like clockwork.

I could see Mom watching the time as the pumpkin pie made its appearance. She had no intention of crossing paths. It's civil between them, albeit a tight-lipped civility. But it's not warm. Callie will not have that cherished photo of her with both her maternal grandparents. That's divorce. The baby will learn.

Dad walked into the house and put two boxes down on the dining room table.

He said, "These are baby things."

Before I could respond, he looked at me a little sheepishly and said, "Well, I haven't really gotten her anything yet."

Chalk up two more gifts—one soft stuffed dog dubbed Grandpa and a peculiarly stretchy iridescent bean-bag bullfrog, which Dad suggested will be very helpful come next spring when the bullfrogs in the pond across the street wake up and begin their wicked-bad harmonizing and the baby demands an explanation.

Frogs we can explain. Human beings are a little trickier.

November 25 — Sunday

QTY/ITEM	CAT	PRICE	TOTAL
10 Enfamil	larger baby — larger bottles	29.90	
4 Gerber jarred food	larger bottles — larger appetite	1.78	
1 Pampers Jumbo, size 3	larger appetite — larger diapers	13.49	
		$45.17	$7,098.50

November 26 — Monday

And so it begins — "the silly season" as father-of-child would say. Here starts foolish spending and high-pressured largesse.

Callie will not be exempt. Welcome to Christmas, baby girl.

In addition to gifts, there is the question of a Christmas card. I have, in the past, sent cards and therefore, I cannot rightly bill Callie for those costs.

Remember, all expenses must pass this simple test: Would I be spending the money if Callie didn't exist?

So, the cards will not be billed. However, the mandatory Christmas photo of the child is another matter, along with the necessary supplies for adhering the photo to the unbillable card.

QTY/ITEM	CAT	PRICE	TOTAL
1 Double-stick tape	photo adhesive	$2.59	$7,101.09

Please know that she will be wearing her new bright-red, hand-smocked-with-Santa-and-reindeer-cross-stitched Christmas dress for the photo. It is an amazing thing to behold and was made for her gratis by her good friend Ann.

November 28 — Wednesday

QTY/ITEM	CAT	PRICE	TOTAL
1 Weight Watchers weekly fee	pain & suffering	$10.55	$7,111.64

Down 2.2 pounds.

Speaking of food — Callie is being put on a breakfast, lunch, and dinner schedule. Though I understand she can be perfectly healthy with nothing more than formula/breast milk for the first year, it has also been suggested to me that the sooner an array of foods is introduced, the more likely she is to try them without a struggle. Therefore, three times a day she will be deposited into her high chair for an official feeding of new and interesting tastes and textures.

Crank up the calculator. Diversity comes at a price.

QTY/ITEM	CAT	PRICE	TOTAL
1 Gerber oatmeal cereal	culinary diversity	1.50	
1 Beechnut Turkey	" "	.79	
1 Gerber turkey	" "	.79	
1 Beechnut chicken	" "	.79	
1 Gerber lamb	" "	.79	
1 Beechnut veal	" "	.79	
1 Beechnut applesauce	" "	.50	
1 Gerber prunes	" "	.45	
1 Gerber peas	" "	.44	
		$6.84	$7,118.48

November 29 — Thursday

Stopped by a children's store in Grand Central. The child's stocking has to be filled, after all.

QTY/ITEM	CAT	PRICE	TOTAL
2 Wooden maracas	stocking stuffer	$6.00 (Comped)*	

*It is Christmas. I do understand the basic concept behind the holiday. I don't intend to charge her for the gifts I purchase for her but I feel it's important to at least note them in the name of public service.

November 30 — Friday

Mom and I popped into Toys "R" Us—there's always something you need.

QTY/ITEM	CAT	PRICE	TOTAL
1 Pack Learning Links	insta-toy retrieval*	1.99	
6 9-oz. bottles	big girl conversion	3.99	
2 Fast-flow nipples	same as above	3.99	
6 Cross-cut nipples	same as same as	2.49	
		$12.46	$7,130.94

This is actually a savings for Callie. It will save me from picking up every last thing she owns when she tosses every last thing she owns onto the floor. Which in turn will save her as she will not be billed for the back surgery I would have been certain to need had I continued to retrieve every last thing she owned off the floor after she had tossed it all there.

The thing about Toys "R" Us stores is that they tend to be very close to Kids "R" Us stores. So mom and I popped in there too.

QTY/ITEM	CAT	PRICE	TOTAL
1 Pair dress shoes	Christmas photo footwear	14.99	
2 Outfits	absolute unjustifiable spending	24.25 (comped)	
		$14.99	$7,145.93

December 1 — Saturday

It has been proclaimed officially by the child's father that after weeks of speculation, the girl as spoken her first word.

It's "kitty."

Not Mama. Not Dada.

Kitty.

I'm a little hurt.

December 2 — Sunday

Let me say this clearly—popping into stores that contain things for babies is a bad habit. You find yourself buying the most peculiar things.

QTY/ITEM	CAT	PRICE	TOTAL
1 Percussive egg rattle	musical training	$2.99	$7,148.92

Of course, one has little choice when it comes to popping into the grocery store.

QTY/ITEM	CAT	PRICE	TOTAL
1 Chicken breast strips	solid food	3.30	
10 Enfamil	liquid food	29.90	
1 Banana	sol-quid food	.65	
5 Jars organic baby food	politically correct food	2.73	
2 Jars regular food	good ol' 'merican food	.89	
		$37.47	$7,186.39

December 3 — Monday

The girl has a tooth! I feel unbelievably proud — of myself for some reason. She has sprouted a tooth and I feel giddy like it's my accomplishment. Perhaps it's kudos to myself for the simple endurance of getting to this point.

December 4 — Tuesday

Something unhealthy is happening to me — or rather to my credit card. It's being overexercised and I seem incapable of bringing it under control.

The frenzied allure of shopping has always eluded me. But while I still have no desire to hit the stores in search of clothing for myself or kitchen utensils or household decor items, these days I cannot hold myself back when I see a Carter's, Baby Gap, Children's Place, or any other boutique that might have anything at all that could be worn by Callie. Or, as it turns out, any baby.

I better understand the syndrome now.

While I was still pregnant, I visited my friend Gabrielle. I sat down at her kitchen table and she pulled out a Baby Gap bag in which were, I kid you not, ten outfits for my unborn baby. I really didn't know what to say. Jesse, Gabrielle's husband, explained that they had considered another baby but weren't going to do it and therefore, somehow that explained why I/Callie had received ten new outfits.

But Jesse was wrong. The cycle is much bigger than that.

Yesterday, Mom and I discovered a very dangerous place — an enormous outlet village only forty minutes from home. Normally, I wouldn't care about such a thing but there is a Carter's Store in this village and a Baby Gap. We never got past the Carter's yesterday (obviously we will be making more trips) because the Carter's is stocked with all the exact items that are in the department stores and everything is at least 50 percent off. Mom and I went racing from corner to corner trying to burn off some of the hyper energy created by this abundance, but the presence of so many tiny outfits only spun us further out of control. Callie stared stoney-eyed into the mayhem.

Today, she has four new outfits, a special new bowl, and a vibrating bug toy.

But more noteworthy, I think, is the fact that my pregnant friends Gale and Carol each have new outfits for their unborn babies as well. Pre-Callie, an impregnated friend would have received from me the A. A. Milne box set — *When We Were*

Young, Now We Are Six, and *The House on Pooh Corner.* It was a lovely and tasteful gift and it meant I didn't have to go to a special store to procure baby clothing and sort through too many badly designed cutesy frills. A set of literary classics was so much cleaner.

Not anymore. Now there are clothes and lots of 'em and here's why:

Because Gabrielle and so many of my other friends shopped so thoroughly for Callie in her early days, I never had the thrill of picking and purchasing those tiniest of clothes and now Callie is light-years beyond them.

So, it's my turn to grab the rush and revisit my baby's youth by buying too many clothes for my pregnant friends. In turn, when their babies are too old to wear the really cute eensy things, they'll chum up with some other pregnant friend and buy too many clothes for them. I don't even know what Gale is having—a boy or a girl—and I still couldn't stop myself from buying for her. I just got everything in green. Imagine when she finds out—I'll have to set aside a full day for a really serious shop.

Mom and I already have plans to go back because there's Laura and Moye to shop for too. (And I should probably also pick up something for Lonnie for Christmas. I'll have to make a quick stop at one of the grown-up stores.)

It's so fortunate that my friends are having babies. Otherwise, I would have to shop for strangers.

QTY/ITEM	CAT	PRICE	TOTAL
1 Booties	Carol	2.40	
1 Jumpsuit	Carol	7.00	
1 Receiving blanket	Carol	7.00	
1 Jumpsuit	Gale	7.00	
1 Cardigan	Gale	7.00	
1 Pant	just in case*	7.80	
1 Shirt	just in case*	7.00	
		$45.20[†]	$7,231.59

*Either Laura's or Moye's baby is bound to be a girl—or if not, it's a given that someone else will get pregnant soon enough. Good to have a spare . . . and it's a really cute set.

[†]I know it's my emotional disorder that is creating this expense but it is a disorder that has emerged due to the baby. These things don't even qualify as replacements for my previous book-set gifts because they aren't official shower or birth gifts. Those will still need to be acquired, A. A. Milne or otherwise.

December 5 — Wednesday

QTY/ITEM	CAT	PRICE	TOTAL
1 Weight Watchers weekly fee	you tell me	$10.55	$7,242.14

Up .6 pounds. I am revamping my goal. I'd like to have this weight off before I retire.

December 6 — Thursday

The following two thoughts are not related. Lonnie ate the baby's banana and I will be forty years old six months from today.

Naturally, I was understanding and handled the banana hijacking like the mature (very) and professional adult that I am. I only worked it into the conversation seven times over the course of fifteen minutes.

Lonnie, on the other hand, didn't handle it as well. After the sixth mention of how he had selfishly eaten the only natural food his daughter could eat — how he had just thoughtlessly popped the fruit between his greedy gums only to leave his infant girl to go without — how he had thought only of his own wants, needs, and desires while his defenseless baby lay innocently gurgling in the living room waiting for a breakfast that would never come — he shouted, "Okay! I get it! I get it! I am really sorry I ate the banana! I'll never, ever do it again."

He is so sensitive.

Meanwhile, I selflessly ran to the store to remedy the calamity.

QTY/ITEM	CAT	PRICE	TOTAL
1 Bunch bananas	replacement	1.32 (reimbursement — no charge)	
2 Enfamil	father-proof food	5.98	
1 Pampers Wipe	plague control	5.79	
		$11.77	$7,253.91

December 7 — Friday

QTY/ITEM	CAT	PRICE	TOTAL
1 Aetna US Healthcare co-pay	insurance	15.29	
1 Vision @ $4.54	insurance	4.54	
		$19.83	$7,273.74

There is a second tooth. It won't be long now before she's going to have to start picking up that dental coverage expense.

There are also more clothes. I went back to that outlet. But I'm not going to list them here. Instead, I will talk the whole thing over with a good therapist. I may have to bill Callie for the therapy but not for all the new clothes. It's just excessive American acquisitional materialism. I'm disgusted by me.

I do believe she should be responsible for her four new barrettes, however. She is the one who opted to grow her hair long enough for it to fall in her eyes. As a result, her bone straight locks are threatening to cause some future vision disturbance if they aren't wrangled. Barrettes in the here-and-now save big-time on glasses and/or eye patches later. Just another example of me looking out for her, trying to limit her debt until she's able to make her own fiscally responsible decisions.

QTY/ITEM	CAT	PRICE	TOTAL
4 Pastel hair clips	optic prophylactic	$2.00	$7,275.74

December 8 — Saturday

My recent forays to the outlet and elsewhere have been made possible by a recent life-altering purchase. I would like to nominate the automobile bottle warmer for "Best Product of the Decade." In the march of progress of our industrialized society, I rank it just below the steam engine, the rocket booster, and the microchip.

QTY/ITEM	CAT	PRICE	TOTAL
1 Gerber automobile bottle warmer	freedom	$16.98	$7,292.72

I can now leave the house with the child almost as if we are ordinary human beings, masters of our own destinies. We do not have to run at breakneck speed in order to be home for the next bottle. We just plug the bottle warmer into the cigarette lighter and tool on down the interstate while the formula heats up and the baby has lunch.

Brilliant.

December 9 — Sunday

QTY/ITEM	CAT	PRICE	TOTAL
1 Banana	breakfast nosh	.40	
1 Squash	favorite food stash	.45	
2 Organic food	hip cuisine	1.09	
10 Cans Enfamil	ye olde standby	29.90	
1 Pampers, size 3	appearances	13.49	
		$45.33	$7,338.05

December 10 — Monday

QTY/ITEM	CAT	PRICE	TOTAL
4 Muffins	baby meeting	$4.79	$7,342.84

The first meeting of the Class of 2019 went off without a hitch yesterday. Callie hosted a visit from Lusanna, her cousin Brierley, and young Liam, who still must devote the majority of his time and energy to keeping his head upright and centered. These are four of the seven children born in my town this year and so it is more than half of the kindergarten class of 2006 — ultimately the high school graduating class of 2019.

I served muffins to Laura, Sara, and Teresa—the PTA. We sat around and watched our babies establish themselves among their peers as, I think, we all enjoyed the relief of de-isolation for an afternoon.

At one point, Laura put Lusanna in the Ultrasaucer, where Lusanna was content to stay.

"This is why I can't have one of these," Laura said, referring to the saucer. "I'd never take her out of it. Look how happy I am." She leaned back against the couch and lifted her tired empty arms into the air. Freedom.

It occurred to me at that moment that these women are my new friends. We will more than likely be in each other's lives in a very real way for a good long time even though, without the babies, we might never have met. Between story hours and Christmas tree lightings and baby meetings, I see these women far more now than I see any of my old pals, who have now been mostly relegated to half-finished phone calls.

It's good, I guess. Now, I have new friends who are as un-available to the rest of life as I am.

December 11 — Tuesday

Callie does not feel my pain.

I record this reality as a warning and a comfort to others.

The warning: Do not expect your children to care.

The comfort: Do not feel alone, others' children do not care either.

It has become clear that despite the life-altering sacrifices Lonnie and I have made in order to bring Callie into this world and to make her stay here as comfortable as possible, she is not particularly appreciative. In fact, it appears her response is nearly always the same. No matter what I say to her, no matter how I try to clarify the ways in which this, my year of deprivation, has affected me, Callie looks at me with an expression that says no more and no less than, "Oh, well."

"Callie, I'm exhausted."

"Oh, well."

"Callie, I'm hungry and fat."

"Oh, well."

"Callie, the tedium of stacking these cups on top of each other so that you can knock them over is wearing me down to a dull nub."

"Oh, well."

"Callie, most of my hair has fallen out and what hasn't fallen out has turned gray."

"Oh, well."

"Callie, I run all day every day—to the city, to the store, around the house, around the office, back to you, after you, for you. I don't have a second to myself."

"Oh, well."

"Callie, I live every day with this buried-deep, ripping pain as my love for you and my fear of ever losing you tears me apart on a cellular level."

"Oh, well."

December 12 — Wednesday

QTY/ITEM	CAT	PRICE	TOTAL
1 Weight Watchers weekly fee	hunger strike	$10.55	$7,353.39

Down 2 pounds—that's 15 pounds altogether now, which means I got applause at the meeting tonight. You get applause every 5 pounds—the girls say, "Oooh" and they clap. I also got myself another "5" sticker to put on Callie's "I Lost Five Pounds" bookmark, too.

Perhaps more significant, however, is the fact that we are in the midst of another round of otitis media.

After two nights of minimal sleep due to the child's constant waking (it's amazing how much of any given night can actually be spent in the action of waking), I decided to take her into the shop, have 'em look under the hood.

Dr. Brown said yup. Mild to moderate. Left ear. So now we're on another ten-day cycle of hot-pink antibiotics that will turn every piece of clothing the child owns into one matching pink ensemble.

Here's a simple question for you—how come they can't come up with an antibiotic that doesn't leave pink on every-thing it touches? I have a hard time believing hot pink is actu-ally the color of the medication. I have a hunch it's not a naturally occurring substance. It has to be there for bubblegum appeal, which is basically lost on my child as she does not, to date, chew a lot of gum being as she has only two teeth in her head and they're not even fully functioning yet. It'll be a while before she's snappin' sassy at the drugstore counter.

Suffice to say, I could live without the pink appeal. I believe if enough parents protest on behalf of eternally pink clothing, linens, and upholstery, we will eventually find ourselves living in a world with the option of white, or better yet transparent, medication.

QTY/ITEM	CAT	PRICE	TOTAL
1 Doctor's visit co-pay	ears	15.00	
1 Bottle pink stain	medication	8.99	
1 Pediacare	back-up	5.79	
1 Infant Tylenol	back-up for back-up	5.59	
1 Gerber bib	stain resistant bib	1.99	
		$37.36	$7,390.75

December 13 — Thursday

I must say, for this her first Christmas, she's getting by on precious little in the gift-giving department. Just passing around photos of herself for the most part. However, even giving of oneself comes at a price.

QTY/ITEM	CAT	PRICE	TOTAL
9 4x6 dupe prints	generosity	9.00	
3 5x7 dupe prints	larger generosity	27.00	
2 8x10 dupe prints	the biggest generosity	20.00	
1 double picture frame	silver-plated generosity	59.36	
		$115.36	$7,506.11

December 15 — Saturday

Despite no signs of real interest, I continue to purchase solid foods for Callie.

I worry she is not progressing apace toward a life of lumpy food and eating utensils. The only thing on the planet she doesn't put in her mouth is Cheerios.

Here is the mental picture I have of her on the first day of kindergarten. She is an extraordinarily cute and well-dressed girl who talks a blue-streak but must be carried from place to place. Upon arriving at each destination, she is placed in the sitting position, where she remains until the next move. Should she need anything between moves, she commands the troupe of cats that follow her wherever she goes and they fetch whatever she requests. She knows the answer to every question before any other child in the room but she always forgets to raise her hand before offering it. At lunch, she is carried into the cafeteria, where she dines on a variety of liquids, all administered through bottles. The last bottle she takes is her daily dose of hot-pink medicine.

She will not rest at naptime—won't even lie down. When asked by her teachers why she won't sleep, she tells them she doesn't need sleep. Not during the day, not at night, never. She is a superhero and her special skill is the ability to live life to its fullest on absolutely no sleep.

QTY/ITEM	CAT	PRICE	TOTAL
10 Enfamil	staple	29.90	
5 Jar food	stage 2—lumpy	2.73	
2 Bananas	slimy toy	.85	
		$33.48	$7,539.59

December 18 — Tuesday

My eyes are burning. I want sleep.

She has waited until now, until the end of her third fiscal quarter, to introduce me to the kind of fatigue I was supposed to experience when she was a newborn—back when she was (relatively speaking) a brilliant sleeper. Now she wakes hourly until midnight and then twice more before morning, meaning 6 A.M. And, of course, as it was and ever shall be, Lonnie would help if he were awake to know what was happening. However, a screeching hyena six inches from his eardrum apparently does not disrupt him.

The only advantage I can see to Callie's postponement of her newborn sleep schedule is that I'm not breast-feeding anymore and therefore, I can get all jacked-up wicked-ugly on six cups o' jo a day.

Sleep is at the bottom of all of it. I see it now. It's the reason we do everything we do—scramble for money, kick and fight our way toward personal accomplishments, get things off our chests. It's all in an effort to sleep well when we're done, in a luxuriously expensive bed hidden away in a warm and secure house with the ease of self-fulfillment and the lightness of a clear conscience.

Just let me sleep. I'd do anything to sleep through the night, to experience that again. It's been so long.

She is nine months and four days old today. She no longer takes a bottle during the night. She has two teeth protruding from her lower gum. She says "kitty" and "tree." When placed on her feet and held by the hands, she takes off across the room with no idea that she can't walk. She has an advanced sense of comic timing.

She will not crawl. She does not eat food. She won't let me sleep.

I really want to sleep. I'm an American after all, and damn it, it is my right and national duty to sleep. Sleep is what defines us. It's what we do best. Work like dogs so we can sleep like the dead. Sleep is death without the inconvenience. So kill me a little.

Sleep is the human condition. It's where we all want to be. One must experience a sizeable interruption if one is to stay from sleeping—an air raid with twenty GIs surrounding your bed shouting *"Incoming"* might work, or maybe trying to catch

forty winks on a bed of nails would be effective. Strobe light-
ing and a flock of ducks on your pillow might also keep you up.

Or you could just move in with us and try living with
my baby.

> *Credits:* $1,680.49
> *Disbursements:* $7,539.59

The Fourth
Fiscal Quarter

~

Speculating Futures

December 19 — Wednesday

There's a lump on the baby.

"I want to send you to a pediatric surgeon," says Dr. Brown yesterday when I showed the lump to him at her nine-month checkup. Then he started talking about embryonic defects and I started to hear an odd buzzing in my ears.

I found the lump two days ago, right in the middle of her collarbone. I made Mom come over at nine o'clock at night because Lonnie wasn't home and I needed someone to tell me it was okay. I called Dad the dermatologist on the phone and described it to him but the only thing a doctor hates more than insurance companies is being asked to diagnose something without seeing it. He did say, however, that he felt that as long as she had an appointment already set for thirty-six hours from that moment, I shouldn't worry. Mom agreed and added that I should leave a message for Dr. Brown as it would make me feel better. Everyone seemed to agree: Thirty-six hours would be soon enough.

And that's true. In reality, nobody thinks this lump is a vicious thing with malign intentions. It is, most likely, some sort of harmless cyst that may even resolve itself. And it doesn't seem to bother her in the slightest. Nonetheless, I do not want it on my baby's body. I want it to leave and I want to stop flashing on scary scenarios. There's so much to fear when a baby is looking to you for everything it wants, desires, and needs. The world turns into one big pitfall.

I have a bad track record with lumps in December. Seven years ago, it was me on December 22. Three years ago, it was Mom on December 24. Now it's Callie, with an appointment with the pediatric surgeon who will assess the situation on December 28.

On the upside, the current events have me far less concerned with the fact that I was up .8 pounds when I weighed in tonight.

QTY/ITEM	CAT	PRICE	TOTAL
1 Weight Watchers weekly fee	hobby	$10.55	$7,550.14

December 21 — Friday

QTY/ITEM	CAT	PRICE	TOTAL
1 Aetna US Healthcare co-pay	insurance	15.29	
1 Vision @ $4.54	insurance	4.54	
		$19.83	$7,569.97

December 23 — Sunday

QTY/ITEM	CAT	PRICE	TOTAL
1 Pampers Mega, size 3	mega important	19.49	
10 Enfamil	mega filler	29.90	
3 Jars baby food	mega fun	1.84	
		$51.23	$7,621.20

December 24 — Monday

Innocent, I tell you. We were innocent as we walked the aisles of Grand Union in search of an angel food cake to go with the berries for Christmas dinner dessert (calorie-conscious version). We were absolutely not looking to procure yet another gift for the child but then, there at the end of aisle 5, right near the coffee and just around from the canned vegetables, was a collection of very cute quacking-mooing-whinnying barnyard animals. Callie charmed the holiday shoppers as she screamed with delight at each of the animals—priced at $8.99 or $6.99, depending on whether you have a Grand Union card. Mom's eyes glazed over as she looked on Callie with adoration. I knew we were lost. We'd be going home with at least one barnyard animal or another. Mom purchased Dani Duck.

I mention this not because I'm going to bill Callie for this gift (it was Gramma's dough, after all) but more as a cautionary tale. Not only did Mom spend the money on Dani but she now intends to return to the Grand Union to obtain for herself a shopping card from said establishment. Then, she intends to purchase the entire collection—eight animals—so she can sing "Old MacDonald" with Callie and they can point to each animal and hear its sound as they sing the song.

Therefore, an unsuspecting visit to the grocery store for a low-cal holiday dessert has turned into one gift purchase and seven more perspective gift purchases. In addition, once my mother begins visiting Grand Union for the various farm animals, she will no doubt pick up a few other grocery items as needed. Grand Union is more expensive than Stop & Shop (which is the reason we rarely go there except for things like angel food cake). But convenience will no doubt win out and Mom will end up spending more on every item purchased there.

This is of even greater concern when you consider the fact that Mom has always been careful with the coin. She has lived her life very modestly and yet, with this baby, she's getting sucker punched left and right. Callie's got her hooks in and knows it. She doesn't turn to me when she sees something she wants on a store shelf. She turns to Gramma and squeals with an extra sparkle in her eye. And she gets what she wants. There's something going on between them, some kind of contracted agreement to which I am not privy. And I don't know as there's any going back. Like any good cult leader, Callie has worked her magic and Mom doesn't even know she's being had.

But perhaps Mom's story can help others. Never lower your guard. Potential baby purchases lurk around every corner and babies know it. And they know where you're vulnerable, they'll show no mercy, they will get what they want. All you can do is keep your head down, eyes fixed on the floor, purchase only those things written on your list in a calm and legible hand. Stray from these guidelines and you will be walking on thin ice, down a slippery slope, upstream without a paddle.

December 25 — Tuesday

The baby has adjusted very nicely to materialism.

With no experience or training, she sat through Christmas morning and accepted gift after gift as if it were her birthright. It took no more than three demonstrations of the empty-hand-into-stocking-full-hand-out-of-stocking maneuver for her to grasp it all.

For her first Christmas she got: a Discovery Toy Activity Box, one dump truck with movable parts, a rubber frog, a collection of bath toys, a box of holiday greeting cards (her father's notion,) a plastic cow, a baby sled, two wooden maracas, a plastic globe air ball, a wood-cut barnyard puzzle with knobs, a plastic yellow car, a Baby Bach Musical Pipes toy, an electric spinning top, a bedtime bear, a pink Amelia Earhart hat with tassel, a pair of casual booties with car motif, two stuffed Clifford dogs, a wooden crèche scene, a Christmas dress, a New Year's Eve black velvet with sequins outfit, one CD, one Christmas cassette tape, one Little Linguist electronic toy, four books (one half-Japanese, one fuzzy), one pair pink mittens with string, one pair pink mittens without string, a Winnie-the-Pooh rattle, three dolls, a matching vest/hat/mitten set, one mother-baby duck toy, two winter outfits, three bank checks, one striped pant/jacket outfit slated to fit when she's three, a My First Phone, a Vermont Teddy Bear in University of Michigan attire, Shelley the Sensory Snail, a large frog puppet that ribbits, and a small stuffed duck that quacks (previously introduced).

Callie's eyes were a bit buggy by the end but other than that, she gave each new toy a good bang and a solid kick and moved on to the next. After a while, she took a quick nap and returned ready for more.

I can only wait for the day when she will be assigned the task of writing her own thank-you notes. That'll put a ripple in her cool reserve, a dent in the side of her already too-thick entitlement veneer.

December 26 — Wednesday

QTY/ITEM	CAT	PRICE	TOTAL
1 Crayola jumbo crayon pack	office supplies	$5.00	$7,626.20

I have decided she is going to help with the thank-you notes. And since I didn't happen to have any cash on me when I was struck with the brilliant notion of providing her with crayons so she could create her own cards, I had to charge the purchase and one cannot charge a mere five-dollar expense. Therefore, I was forced to purchase a really adorable pair of ridiculously expensive tights in a European size so you *know* they're hip.

QTY/ITEM	CAT	PRICE	TOTAL
1 Supremely hip pair of tights	cash-flow problems	$20.00	$7,646.20

December 27 — Thursday

QTY/ITEM	CAT	PRICE	TOTAL
1 Weight Watchers weekly fee	reduction	$10.55	$7,656.75

Down 2 pounds. Another 9.8 pounds and Callie will be done paying for her share of my expansion. I will have returned to the weight I was when I first weighed in at the doctor's office after figuring out I was pregnant. (Though I suspect I was already up several pounds by then since my body seemed to take to pregnancy like a sponge to water.) I feel strongly that

I should reach this particular goal weight by Callie's first birthday; it would be too depressing not to.

Her doctor's appointment is tomorrow.

December 28 — Friday

Dad on the phone says, "Now you have to play the role of brave mom who doesn't transmit fear to the child. That'll be your hardest job."

Here's the lowdown: There's no getting around it, Callie will have surgery to remove her lump. She will be under a general anesthesia and will have a small scar when all is said and done. We will either keep her well supplied with beautiful necklaces to perfectly camouflage the mark or stock her wardrobe with V-necks that will feature the scar like a medal of honor — depending on the girl she grows into being. I'm betting on the V-necks.

Blessedly, everyone agrees this is a benign little lump and once it's gone it will be gone. The bullet will be dodged. Although, as has been pointed out to me by more than one friend, once you have a child, there's always a bullet out there. You have to keep ducking and moving.

We must now spend one more week getting three doses of pink medicine down the child's throat each day with the hopes of reducing the lump to as small a mass as possible. Then we will visit the doctor again and schedule the surgery.

As we were leaving our appointment today, Callie was given a brand-new toy to take home — a Fisher-Price Play Desk. My first reaction, while impressed with the largesse of the doctor's practice, was that I didn't even want to bring the thing into the house. It was clearly one of many toys donated for "sick children" at the holidays, the ones stuck in hospitals over Christmas. Callie is not a sick baby. She's just got a lump. But in the end, I've decided it's her toy and she has a right to use it or not as she pleases. It's her prize for doing battle.

So, although she has a cyst that requires surgery and will leave a scar, she has obtained a $17.00 toy free of charge. She seems fine with the arrangement.

QTY/ITEM	CAT	PRICE	TOTAL
1 Doctor's co-pay	lump	20.00	
1 Antibiotic	delumping	8.79	
		$28.97	$7,685.72

December 29 — Saturday

QTY/ITEM	CAT	PRICE	TOTAL
1 Bottle fluoride	dental	5.00	
12 Enfamil	maintenance	36.08	
1 Gerber 2-handle cup	leak prevention	4.39	
1 Pampers Mega, 3	same as above	16.98	
1 Pampers Wipes	cleaning supplies	4.98	
3 Jars veggies	eating practice	2.05	
1 Gerber Graduate Biscuits	teeth practice	1.99	
		$71.47	$7,757.19

December 30 — Sunday

I forgot to mention that I forgot to bring a bottle when we made the drive to the surgeon's office on Friday. Therefore, it became necessary to pick up a four-pack of Enfamil ready-made. True, it was my forgetfulness that brought about the purchase but the only reason I forgot is because I was supposed to remember. If Callie didn't need the bottle, I wouldn't have forgotten it because I wouldn't have needed to remember it.

QTY/ITEM	CAT	PRICE	TOTAL
1 4-pack Enfamil	short-term memory	$6.59	$7,763.78

December 31 — Monday

Today, I packed up the Little Linguist and returned it to its manufacturer. It's the first broken Christmas toy in what I am sure will be a long line of breaking toys. The Little Linguist, in theory, is a very cool machine, especially for a child whose father insists on reading Clifford to her in Spanish every morning over rice cereal and bananas. (For the record, Lonnie doesn't speak much more Spanish than Callie does. They're studying together.)

The Little Linguist is a round disc-shaped machine with a receptor port in its center that fits twenty different plastic characters and objects such as a "monkey," "bear," "house," "cow," and so on. When you place one of these objects in the center receptor port, the Little Linguist tells you the name of the object in keeping with the disc that is inserted—English, Spanish, French, German, or Japanese. Then if you press a second button, it gives you a sample of the sound that thing makes.

I installed the batteries, inserted the Spanish disc, and deposited the cat, or "gato," into the receptor.

The machine said "elephante" and barked.

I took the batteries out, packed up all the parts, and sent it back with a note detailing the machine's confusion and instructing the manufacturer that I would like a replacement machine if this is atypical of its behavior. However, if the Little Linguist has a tendency toward instructing small children that in Mexico trees are called casas and if you listen carefully you can hear them oinking—then I would just prefer a refund.

QTY/ITEM	CAT	PRICE	TOTAL
1 Return postage	linguistic anarchy	$7.70	$7,771.48

January 2 — Wednesday

QTY/ITEM	CAT	PRICE	TOTAL
1 Weight Watchers weekly fee	reduction	$10.55	$7,782.03

Down .6 pounds. Another few years and I should have the weight situation under control.

January 4 — Friday

QTY/ITEM	CAT	PRICE	TOTAL
1 Aetna US Healthcare			
co-pay	insurance	15.29	
1 Vision @ $4.54	insurance	4.54	
		$19.83	$7,801.86

January 5 — Saturday

Dear Sir or Madam:

My nine-month-old granddaughter is delighted with her seven farmyard friends, which we have purchased in a variety of grocery stores in the area. I understand there are eight animals in the collection but don't know which one we are missing. The stores tell us they were holiday promotional items and they don't expect to receive any more. We would very much like to complete our farmyard and wonder if we can order the missing friend from you.

Our current collection:

Dani Duck   Freddie Frog
Kassie Kitten   Cosey Cow
Peeke Pig   Pepi Puppy
Paco Pony

I would appreciate any information you can provide to help us complete our collection.

Thank you.

Mary Lou Howie

January 6 — Sunday

The baby's bump is getting bigger. I called the surgeon earlier today and he said, "Put her back on the antibiotic, continue the warm soaks four times a day, and if it's not better by morning, I'll see you here at the hospital."

He also said she cannot eat anything more than Pedialyte from midnight on, on the chance that she needs to be put under general anesthesia. And she cannot eat at all within two hours of arriving at the hospital.

This should be fun.

QTY/ITEM	CAT	PRICE	TOTAL
1 4-pack unflavored Pedialyte	pre-surgical food	5.19	
8 Cans Enfamil	post-surgical food	23.92	
1 Gerber Teething Biscuit	fun food	1.59	
7 Large jars food	lumps	4.67	
3 Small jars food	bumps	1.50	
		$36.87	$7,838.73

January 7—Monday

QTY/ITEM	CAT	PRICE	TOTAL
1 4-pack Cherry Pedialyte	improved palatability	5.99	
1 Tylenol with codeine	pain management	9.49	
1 Bottle peroxide	infection control	.69	
1 Package cotton balls	dressing	1.49	
1 Pack large band-aid pads	dressing	4.79	
		$22.45	$7,861.18

January 9—Wednesday

QTY/ITEM	CAT	PRICE	TOTAL
1 Weight Watchers weekly fee	whatever	$10.55	$7,871.73

Up .4 pounds. Whatever.

QTY/ITEM	CAT	PRICE	TOTAL
1 Pack medium Band-Aid pads	dressing, round two	3.99	
1 Bottle prune juice	narcotic antidote liquid	.60	
1 Jar prunes	narcotic antidote solid	.50	
		$5.09	$7,876.82

January 10 — Thursday

The baby no longer has a bump. Now it is a deep incision that must be cleaned and dressed daily with a prayer to keep away infection so that we can finally be done with this.

We arrived at the Children's Medical Center in Hartford at 10:00 A.M. on Monday morning. By 12:45 P.M., I was holding Callie down on the operating table as a plastic gas mask was placed over her nose and mouth and her muffled cry burrowed itself into my permanent psyche, where it will be available for all time to haunt me.

After she was out, I was escorted to the waiting room. For the first time in Callie's life, she was not under the direct care of me, her father, or her grandmother. And she handled it like a champ. She is a super-baby with very special powers.

However, I am just an ordinary mortal and I had a hard time with this, but I will not overplay it. It was not fun and I wish she didn't have to go through it, but this is a million miles away from any one of the dozen nightmare stories that passed us in those corridors on the way up to Pediatric Day Surgery.

January 11 — Friday

Dear Mrs. Howie:

Thank you for your interest in our products. Our Old MacDonald's Farmyard Friends (Chenille) line is new. If you would like a brochure containing the Chenille Farm program please contact customer service with your name and address. The brochure will be sent through U.S. mail. Please allow one to two weeks for delivery. The missing animal from your collection is Randy Rooster! Sorry for any inconvenience this may have caused. Let us know if we can be of further assistance.

QTY/ITEM	CAT	PRICE	TOTAL
1 Aetna US Healthcare co-pay	insurance	15.29	
1 Vision @ $4.54	insurance	4.54	
		$19.83	$7,896.65

January 12 — Saturday

Finding just the right way to redress an open wound on a baby, complete with a thorough dousing of hydrogen peroxide, is difficult.

QTY/ITEM	CAT	PRICE	TOTAL
1 Pack small Band-Aid pads	re-redressing	3.19	
1 Tube Polysporin	infection control	5.49	
		$8.68	$7,905.33

I try to casually pull the old bandage off while walking around the kitchen with her. My hope is that she won't notice but it doesn't work. She catches on and begins to scream about midway through the de-sticking. So then I have to lay her down and Mom holds her hands as I push up her chin and get the job done. Every day I use a smaller bandage since the tape is as big a problem as anything.

I keep going to the drugstore, certain that if I look hard enough I'll find something to make this easier on my baby. But I haven't found anything. So, instead, I dwell on the fact that she is healing well and then I go to the grocery store and buy her new and interesting things to eat.

QTY/ITEM	CAT	PRICE	TOTAL
1 Box Rice Cereal w/ bananas	interesting breakfast	1.79	
1 Stage 2 Carrots/ Brown Rice	intriguing Lunch	.67	
1 Stage 3 Vegetable Medley	advanced snack	.89	

continued on next page

continued from previous page			
1 Stage 2 Squash/ Corn/Chicken	curious Dinner	.67	
1 Gerber Arrowroot Cookies	tasty dessert	1.39	
8 Cans Enfamil	ye olde standby	23.92	
		$29.33	$7,934.66

January 13 — Sunday

Dad called this afternoon. I was working at my desk and casually picked up the phone to have a conversation of whatever length I cared to have. I leaned back, sipped my coffee, and stared heavy-lidded out the window.

"I'm home alone," I said. Then I giggled. I couldn't help it.

Lonnie is in Chicago and rather than Mom coming here to watch Callie, I took Callie to Mom's. That was a great idea.

"You're all by your lonesome?" Dad asked.

"Yeah," I answered. "And I *really* like being lonesome."

It was alarming when I stopped to count how many months it'd been since I was last alone in my own house. When it finally happened, when I turned around and no one was there, I became giddy with possibility.

I turned on the stereo really loud and belted out show tunes. I had the TV going at the same time but muted just because I could. I leapt around the kitchen and shoved every last thing in my mouth that I wanted to because no one was watching and wondering, on my behalf, just how many points I might be consuming.

I remember now. I liked living alone.

I called Tory to tell her what I had discovered. I wanted to be sure she knew.

"Oh, yeah," she said. "I know. It's great. I remember April called me when Sam was about two and she said, 'You gotta try this!'"

Obviously, it's a well-known secret, passed from parent to parent. Do whatever you have to but figure out a way to be home alone. It occurs to me that not so many months ago I told Lonnie he could no longer make his regular theater-related treks to Chicago because it was just too much for me to be left on my own. I must be sure to let him know I've changed my mind. It's good for him to go out into the world, I think. It's important to travel and learn things. He should go as often as he needs to and maybe more.

January 14 — Monday

She is a ten-month-old baby today. To mark the occasion and celebrate her father's safe return from Chicago, we went out to dinner. She was splendidly behaved sitting in her tabletop clamp-on chair.

Lonnie had the fried oysters. I had the sushi. Callie had the Cheerios.

January 15 — Tuesday

Dammit! Dammit! Dammit! I was taking a noonday stroll down Broadway, walking down the street, minding my own business, when this woman appeared, standing in a doorway holding a small baby in the cradle position. Out of nowhere, absolutely unguided by me, I was flooded with this deep need to reach out and take that tiny baby from her, to hold it and make sure it was safe.

I do not want another one!

I have screamed up and down at a hundred different people who have said, "You have to have another, just wait. When Callie's a little bigger, you're going to miss holding something that small."

I do not want another one and I do not want to want another one! I want to not want another one.

But there it was, an impulse so clear—reach out and take that baby and hold it close to feel that feel. The first signaling of some kind of genetic coding triggered by baby number one—far beyond anything I can control—a prehistoric urge to feel again what I have now felt before.

Dammit! There is a God and its name is biology!

January 16 — Wednesday

The child crawls! It's official. She has independently placed herself in the hands/knees position and moved from point A to point B. Ten months old and she's off and crawling—she's clearly gifted. In recognition of the achievement, Mom and I are taking her to the Carter's outlet to find the perfect crawling outfit, one that hangs just right when you're on all fours.

QTY/ITEM	CAT	PRICE	TOTAL
1 Print turtleneck	crawling outfit	9.10	
1 Print pant	crawling outfit	9.10	
1 Coordinated jacket	crawling outfit	13.10	
		$31.30	$7,965.96

As long as we're on the subject of crawling —

QTY/ITEM	CAT	PRICE	TOTAL
1 Weight Watchers weekly fee	crawling reduction	$10.55	$7,976.51

Down .8 pounds. This is becoming an examination on the nature of "slow."

January 17 — Thursday

We have come upon another costly developmental stage. These are the things she now does completely on her own: sits up, crawls, stands, and cruises (the official term for moving through a space by way of clinging to one large object after another).

Her new abilities have made for a great deal of reorganization. Now we must look at all furniture as a potential clifflike hazard. Every height is now a place from which Callie could take a full-scale header.

Therefore, we have moved her crib mattress down to the second lowest setting so she looks like Kilroy when she pulls herself up to standing and peers over the top of the railing. And Gramma lowered the Pack'n'Play that has served as crib at her house from the "bassinet" position to the "playpen" position. Unfortunately, Callie was deeply offended by the move. She refused to sleep on anything so close to the ground. Therefore, we were forced to purchase an actual crib for Gramma's house.

QTY/ITEM	CAT	PRICE	TOTAL
1 LOV* Fold-a-Way portable crib	header patrol	125.72	
1 Portable crib sheet	anti-header bedding	13.47	
		$139.19	$8,115.70

*That's spelled with three letters and the middle one is a heart.

The Pack'n'Play moved to my house, where it has taken the place of Callie's swing in the living room. She used to love that swing. Now she considers it some kind of POW torture device. When I attempt to put her in the swing she looks at me as if I am a fully diagnosed moron who doesn't understand that she crawls now and has absolutely no room in her schedule for things designed for an infant. Therefore, I have placed the swing on the screened-in porch and will wait for spring to do anything so radical as give it away. She may like it again when the warm spring breezes blow.

In any case, the playpen now sits in front of the fireplace. That kills two birds with one stone. It gives me a handy place to stash the child in crucial moments such as bathroom breaks and it blocks a primary point of baby interest in the room.

My living room now contains no fireplace and one playpen. The look of that is somehow more startling than all the other changes my house has endured over the last year. A playpen in the living room—the house is no longer primarily for adults, even though adults are primarily who live here.

QTY/ITEM	CAT	PRICE	TOTAL
1 Jumbo Pack Pampers	jumbo absorption	27.99	
1 400-pack wipes	jumbo sanitation	9.99	
		$37.98	$8,153.68

January 18—Friday

QTY/ITEM	CAT	PRICE	TOTAL
1 Aetna US Healthcare co-pay	insurance	15.29	
1 Vision @ $4.54	insurance	4.54	
		$19.83	$8,173.51

January 19 — Saturday

Callie used her Christmas sled for the first time today. She was monumentally underwhelmed. I strapped her in and walked back and forth across the yard waiting for her to squeal with glee.

She stared at me the entire time, making clear her thought, "And this is fun—why?"

Perhaps she's waiting for a hill.

January 20 — Sunday

QTY/ITEM	CAT	PRICE	TOTAL
10 Enfamil	the be-all-and-end-all	29.90	
5 Jars food	assorted amusements	2.50	
		$32.40	$8,205.91

January 22 — Tuesday

It's the classic mantra, the one you hear from all parents of young children: "We never see movies anymore."

I was determined not to chant the mantra. I love movies, always have. My mother used to drop me off at the multiplex theater on Saturday morning and pick me up in time for dinner. I would spend the whole day going from theater to theater watching whatever movie was playing, all genres, any topic, various languages. I could find something to enjoy in each of them.

I was adamant, pre-Callie, that I would not relinquish my movie habit. We could work it out. My mother would take care of her or Lonnie could take care of her. We could get a baby-sitter. There are ways to get two hours away to see a movie.

Of course, that was before I was face up against the anxiety and guilt that blossoms every time I leave her. The push-me-pull-you of "I want to get away and have my own life but the baby's face haunts me whenever I leave her" makes it very difficult to prance off to something as unnecessary as a movie. On the other hand, it makes sense to get away when I can. Or so the experts say.

So I have—twice this year.

In both cases, there were hours of vacillating before the decision was made. The first time was early last summer when Lonnie and I left Callie with my mom for the first time to go see *A.I.*

Having little time to read reviews, I didn't really know what the movie was about beyond the fact that a robot boy was the lead character and it was the hip new Spielberg née Kubrick must-see. I did not realize that the entire movie was a tormented search for mother love.

It was not a comfortable two hours.

The very second the credits rolled, I turned to Lonnie and said, "Can we please go home now?!"

Lonnie and I sprang from our seats and raced home to our baby.

It took until yesterday to recover from that episode. Finally, six months later, I made the choice to see another movie. This

time, Lonnie offered to stay with Callie so I could wander off
to the movie on my own. It sounded good on paper but of
course, as soon as I drove away the anxiety began. I practiced
deep breathing and by the time I purchased my ticket, I was
ready to sit down and fall into another world. Tell me a story —
that's what I say to the screen.

I stared ahead and waited for *In the Bedroom* to begin.

Why couldn't someone have told me that the entire movie
centers on parents who lose their child to a violent death?

I should no longer be allowed to pick the movies I see.

I informed Lonnie of this upon my return home. I said, "I
think I'll stick with Disney from here on out."

But it has occurred to me since making that declaration that
Disney might not work either. *Bambi* could kill me.

Is the whole world fueled by mother love?

Don't answer that. I can't take the pressure.

QTY/ITEM	CAT	PRICE	TOTAL
1 Year's worth of movie tickets, 1/week	credit	+ $442.00	($2,122.49)

January 23 — Wednesday

QTY/ITEM	CAT	PRICE	TOTAL
1 Weight Watchers weekly fee	self-worth	$10.55	$8,216.45

Down 2.0. This was a big week at Weight Watchers. I have lost 19.2 pounds.

I have also reached a new power of ten: a new second digit in the number that is my weight. I will not say which power of ten but I will say that it has been a long time since I have been here. In addition, I got my Weight Watcher key chain. This is bestowed upon members when they lose a certain percentage of their weight — I will not say how much as you could easily do the necessary calculations. Suffice to say that I am only 6 pounds from where I was when I first got pregnant.

Most significantly, I have at last lost more than the baby weighs.

January 27 — Sunday

QTY/ITEM	CAT	PRICE	TOTAL
10 Enfamil	staple	29.90	
9 Jars food	increased fruits	4.98	
1 Box Zwieback	in-store snack	1.49	
1 Enfamil 4-pack	full strength back-up	6.59	
1 First Years TV remote	yours/mine training	6.99	
		$49.95	$8,266.41

January 28 — Monday

It is unseasonably warm, the kind of January weather that holds a certain cruelty at its heart. I can hear the creek across the street trickling past the ice and I can smell a moistness in the air that is supposed to coincide with tulips breaking through the ground.

One must be strong, though. One cannot give into a lightness of heart or one will be crushed like a bug beneath the mountainous ridged weight of ice and snow that is sure to bury us all by morning or evening or the next day. I cannot tell you when because I cannot bring myself to turn on the Weather Channel. But I am near forty now and too old and wise to think it might be anything less than soon and with a resounding thud.

Callie had her postsurgical checkup on Friday and we are in a holding pattern. It is uncertain whether she will have to endure a second procedure, uncertain whether that second small lump the surgeon discovered is a swollen gland or another cyst, uncertain whether the darkness beneath the scar will fade on its own. And so, we wait in the unseasonably springlike weather. We have another appointment scheduled with the surgeon for March 8. That seemed like a distant and springlike date until I looked on the calendar and realized that March 8 is only six weeks away. And only six days after that, Callie will have her first birthday.

Now, it's not clear which is more certainly cruel — that winter is far from over or that it's not.

I understand now that the grinding fatigue of this first year is a small gift from God. It puts little stop marks between each minute on the clock so that you are fully aware of every blessed second as you painfully and agingly strain to keep up with an ever-increasingly mobile child. Without that huge and rusting slab of fatigue to jam into the cogs of time, life would go by so fast that we would collectively lose our minds to an unceasing sense of cheated loss, the party going by so quickly there's no time to dance before the band goes home.

I have been trying to get to Toys "R" Us for several days now because I must buy a gate to block the top of the stairs against a now fully automated but uncoordinated individual. I am researching various types of picket fence in order to ensure that a summertime toddler stays far from the dangerous road in front of our house. I am packing more work into my baby-free hours because it is clear that I am no longer on the "she-just-had-a-kid-handle-her-gently" list at work and so now I must run as fast as everyone else, kid or no kid. And I am finding myself staring at the calendar and wondering when one begins the coordination of a first birthday party.

My baby's first year is almost over.

No wonder spring feels like it must hurry. It understands the nature of things far better than I do. Summer, no doubt, is chomping at its heels, telling it to get its ass in gear or it'll roll right past it and spring will never see the light of day—much less dance.

January 30 — Wednesday

The best part of getting baptized is that you get to buy a new outfit.

QTY/ITEM	CAT	PRICE	TOTAL
1 Ivory dress	baptismal wear	72.00	
1 Pair ivory slippers	baptismal footwear	30.00	
		$102.00	$8,368.41

Finding the perfect dress and accompanying shoes was much easier than coming to a sound philosophical and spiritual decision about whether Callie would be baptized at all. However, once the decision was made, it was very clear to me that God would not want her to wear her Thanksgiving dress, and the Christmas dress was out of the question. She does have a lovely linen number but linen really won't do for February and her birthday dress is obviously for her birthday.

So I have selected the prettiest of near-white dresses. It is hand-smocked with little florettes throughout the smocking. It has a beautiful sash and is, of course, lined.

My friend Ann questions billing for this item but I argued that I am not the one getting baptized and the baby has to wear something.

"What about her Thanksgiving shoes?" Ann asked. "Couldn't she at least have worn those? I just don't think you should bill her for $102.00. It doesn't seem fair."

Well, I appreciate the sentiment and the fact that she is concerned for the child's financial future but wearing her Thanks-giving shoes with her baptismal dress is nothing short of ridiculous. They're black. One cannot wear black to a bap-tism — or with a white dress for that matter. Until today, Callie didn't own a single pair of light-colored shoes except the ones with a cow pattern on them and they would be all wrong. I don't see as I had much of a choice.

As for the baptism, Mom is the one who will actually take the vows. We will stand together but Mom will hold the baby and answer the pastor's questions. After witnessing several bap-tisms in the past months and listening very carefully, I decided I could not in good conscience agree to recite and respond with all the words necessary to complete the ceremony. I cannot say "I believe" as much as I believe I would feel a relief if I did.

But Callie deserves to make her own informed decision and so we are going to church. She will learn the stories and the prayers and the songs. She will be baptized. And it may be that in the course of things, she will find that she has the relief of belief.

January 31 — Thursday

Well, that was short-lived. After having celebrated the fact that I had finally lost more than the baby weighed, I took her to the doctor today for some vaccinations and grabbed a minute to put her on the scale.

She weighs 19.2 pounds.

As you may recall, that is the exact amount I have lost after more than three months on Weight Watchers. I find this very peculiar and am beginning to suspect that the child has a nasty competitive streak.

Her weight gain is not the only indicator.

While waiting for Dr. Brown to load up his syringes with life-saving serums, I recounted to him the events of Tuesday night.

Upon returning from a day in the city, toiling away to provide for my baby, I was greeted at my mother's door with a suspicious look and within minutes, howling screams. Every time I tried to pick the baby up, she would reach for my mother and cry so insistently that her lips turned blue. Then she would burrow into my mother and wrap her little arms around her.

This is perhaps the most devastating thing that has ever happened to me.

Callie was seriously pissed off—at me. My mother and Lonnie tried to convince me that she was tired, not feeling well, teething, having a bad hair day, whatever. But Callie and I knew. I have been leaving her with Gramma too much and she is pissed.

Later, after finally getting her into the car, into the house, and into bed, I reconsidered. It is not possible, I told myself, for a 10½-month-old to understand how deeply she could pain me by nuzzling into my mother and refusing to make me the center of her world. It must be something else.

Dr. Brown said, "Oh yes. Oh, yes, she could."

And she did.

Let's not even discuss how many Viennese psychoanalysts it would take to unbury the layers and layers of familial dust loaded up on this scenario—my mother, me, the baby, Callie's mother, my daughter, my mother's daughter, two mothers, one baby, two daughters, one mother—this could be the longest dangling decimal in the world. Let's just say, the situation is loaded.

But Callie got what she wanted. I kept her with me all day long today except for the hour that I snuck away to Weight Watchers . . . where I was down .2 pounds.

I have now lost 19.4 pounds!

Don't mess with me, kid.

QTY/ITEM	CAT	PRICE	TOTAL
1 Weight Watchers weekly fee	competitive edge	$10.55	$8,378.96

February 1—Friday

This morning I woke up and realized that Callie has now experienced one of every month of the year—just one of those morning thoughts.

QTY/ITEM	CAT	PRICE	TOTAL
1 Aetna US Healthcare co-pay	insurance	15.29	
1 Vision @ $4.54	insurance	4.54	
		$19.83	$8,398.79

She should be relieved to pay the above-mentioned insurance costs. Otherwise, she would have been saddled with this:

QTY/ITEM	CAT	PRICE	TOTAL
Pharmacy		5.40	
Med-surg supplies		174.05	
Laboratory		117.53	
Operating rm. serv.		525.76	
Ambul surg care		245.00	
Recovery room		378.42	
		$1446.16	

Instead, she is paying this:

QTY/ITEM	CAT	PRICE	TOTAL
1 Medical co-pay	post-insurance balance	$20.00	$8,418.79

February 2 — Saturday

Randy the Rooster arrived at my mom's house today.
    Callie does not like him.

February 3 — Sunday

QTY/ITEM	CAT	PRICE	TOTAL
10 Enfamil	preferred cuisine	29.90	
1 Gerber Apple Crisp	crunchy cuisine	1.99	
1 Gerber Teething Biscuit	good fun	1.59	
7 Jars assorted food	finger paint	3.88	
		$37.36	$8,456.15

February 4 — Monday

QTY/ITEM	CAT	PRICE	TOTAL
1 Suction bowl	stationary dining	$4.99	$8,461.14

February 5 — Tuesday

Sunday's the big B-day. Had I thought about the fact that we'd be picking up the tab on flowers and had I known that pastors, priests, reverends, and all those, I gather, who are sanctioned to officiate over this business actually get a kickback on services rendered, I might have restrained myself a bit regarding the fashion of the day.

As Callie would say, "Oh, well."

QTY/ITEM	CAT	PRICE	TOTAL
2 Pink rose arrangements	church decor	60.00	
1 Pastoral payoff	sacred kickback	$?? (TBD)	
		$60.00+?	$8,521.14

February 6 — *Wednesday*

Mom's in charge of determining the going rate for baptisms. She wants to absorb the cost, give Callie a break, a gift for joining up.

Lonnie and I have decided to ask Fred and Julie to act as goshparents. They cannot be godparents as I do not want to make a mockery of anyone's beliefs and to truly be a godparent means to take on the possible responsibility of ensuring a Christian education for the child in question should anything happen to the original construct. Fred and Julie aren't going to do that. Honestly, I don't know anyone who would.

But I still want Callie to have the benefit of a second pair of watchful and adoring eyes at school plays and softball games and graduations. I want her to have the notion of godparents — and so I am assigning goshparents.

Fred and Julie live nearby. They are interesting and interested people who laugh a lot and read good books. Fred knows how to build things, identify a fine antique, and fly fish for hours. Julie makes dinners to die for and glows with a yoga radiance. She is a born nurturer. She also used to be married to Lonnie. But never mind.

They will make fine goshparents.

February 7 — Thursday

QTY/ITEM	CAT	PRICE	TOTAL
1 Weight Watchers weekly fee	drudgery	$10.55	$8,531.69

Not up not down — exactly the same. I have been less than 1 pound from 20 pounds for three weeks now. I want my next "5" sticker for my bookmark, dammit. (I mean, Callie's bookmark.)

Perhaps it was my disappointment in not attaining that sticker goal that prompted me to announce to the meeting that I wore nonelastic pants on Tuesday for the first time since August of 2000. For that, I received applause and a star-shaped sticker that says "bravo."

February 9 — Saturday

QTY/ITEM	CAT	PRICE	TOTAL
10 Enfamil	dining & entertainment	29.90	
3 Bananas	mushy potassium	.58	
7 Jars assorted food	fast food for babies	4.07	
1 Gerber's Banana Cookies	change is good	1.59	
		$36.14	$8,567.83

February 11 — Monday

When I have been too glib, I will admit it.

I admit it.

Callie was baptized yesterday and I had to look away because my throat went tight and my eyes began to sting. Of course, it did not happen at the moment of the water and the oil. No. At that moment, I was too busy to be overcome. I was desperately and subtly trying to convince my daughter to relinquish a white plastic container of dental floss given to her by her friend and neighbor, Gloria, a moment before we were called before the congregation. Gloria was only trying to help, attempting to quell a rather noisy bout of fussiness. She pulled the first thing out of her purse she could find. We didn't, in that split second, consider the fact that Callie would not want to leave the fascinating floss in the pew when she ventured forth to join the army of Christ. But she didn't.

So I quietly wrestled with her as the pastor spoke his blessings and poured water from a shell over her head. If I couldn't get it away from her, I at least wanted to turn it around so the congregation couldn't read the words "Dental Floss" on the container. I hoped they might believe it was a special white baptismal teething ring.

For the record, I never did succeed in procuring the item and thus, Lonnie and I not only live with a newly sanctified Lutheran baby but also with a particularly blessed container of dental floss sure to cure the most vicious gum irritation.

So it was not the actual baptism that left me groping for my glib urban pride. It was something intangible hanging in the air several moments before that. A split second between song and preach when I looked around me and saw us.

We were standing in a pew in the tiniest of simple churches in a small New England town surrounded by people I don't really know but have come to recognize. Callie and me, her Gramma and Dad and four friends (goshparents among them) who are not religious but who recognized this event as an important moment and so they wanted to be there to witness and sing and touch the baby's cheek when it was over. I saw Callie looking more radiant than I have ever seen her. She was wearing her $102 dress and shoes with style. But more significant, I suspect, was the golden white jacket and hat that had been knit for me by my grandmother four decades ago that Mom recently pulled from a trunk and carefully washed. When she saw Callie in it, she said, "I hope Non is looking down."

Somewhere in all that, I had to turn my head and look past the frosted glass until I could no longer feel a wetness on my lashes or a caught breath in my throat.

I still do not believe in the story but I'd have to be a fool not to believe in the power it inspires.

The baby is officially Lutheran.

In celebration, we took our friends to breakfast at Callie's favorite restaurant, where the waiters and waitresses vie for her attention.

QTY/ITEM	CAT	PRICE	TOTAL
1 Baptism breakfast	holy pancake	35.79	
1 Container dental floss	blessed replacement	3.49	
		$39.28	$8,607.11

February 13 — Wednesday

Ladies — are you tired of dusting off your child after she's crawled across the dining room floor?

Are you ready to put an end to embarrassing visits from the neighbors whereupon they mistake your baby for a dust kitty?

Then you're ready for the Swiffer!

It's the fabulous electrically-charged magno pick-up system. It's a mop and more! It pulls so much crap off your floor, we can't even really explain it! It's got something to do with static electricity and scientifically approved ions but who cares? It works! It dusts, it sweeps, it makes it much less offensive when your baby licks the linoleum!

So, try it today, ladies — the Swiffer! Available at your local grocers.

QTY/ITEM	CAT	PRICE	TOTAL
1 Swiffer starter kit ·	crawl clean	10.99	
1 Swiffer replace cloths	continued crawl clean	4.99	
		$15.98	$8,623.09

February 14 — Thursday

QTY/ITEM	CAT	PRICE	TOTAL
1 Weight Watchers weekly fee	competitive edge	$10.55	$8,633.64

Down .2 pounds.

Happy Valentine's Day and welcome to Plateauville, where nothing ever changes.

Frustration over my weight loss — or lack thereof — was finally significant enough yesterday that I approached Susan, our fearless leader. She carefully reviewed my daily food journal and I knew where I would get nailed.

Here's the thing — I'm a little bit compulsive. Have I mentioned that? A bit addictive. Perhaps you've noticed. And one of the places where those disorders can work themselves out is at breakfast.

The five mornings of the week when I am not on a train headed for the city, Callie and I suit up and head off to our favorite place in the world, Mountainside Café. We are very popular there. Well, Callie is very popular and I'm the one who carries her so I get caught up in her glow. Anyway, every morning we go to Mountainside and I order one pancake with syrup, no butter. This is not a cheat — I count the points. I am well within my allotted range. However, doing the same thing almost every day for a year is a real red flag here in Plateauville. You have to change it up every now and then. I knew that's what Susan was going to say. She was going to make me give up my pancake and with it a fair portion of my sense of well-being. That pancake gives me ten minutes every day where I don't feel deprived—of food, of sleep, of time, of space.

Perhaps I have asked too much of my pancake.

"Why don't you try a little protein in the morning?" Susan said gently.

I have to do this. Callie is eleven months old today. I have one more month to lose six more pounds if I want to hit my Callie birthday goal.

Egg white omlettes. Pathetic.

QTY/ITEM	CAT	PRICE	TOTAL
1 Tommy Toot	Valentine gift	$6.50 (comped)	

February 15—Friday

QTY/ITEM	CAT	PRICE	TOTAL
1 Aetna US Healthcare co-pay	insurance	15.29	
1 Vision @ $4.54	insurance	4.54	
1 Swing Lock gate	anti-stair-craft	29.99	
		$49.82	$8,683.46

February 16 — Saturday

QTY/ITEM	CAT	PRICE	TOTAL
1 *Big World Atlas* book	Mom-friendly toy*	6.99	
4 Jars assorted food	solid nutrients	2.16	
		$9.15	$8,692.61

*Call it an impulse buy if you want but just because I bought it at the grocery store, between sliced bread and canned fruits, doesn't mean it's not a perfectly good educational item. Besides, I love maps. I can look at them for hours. And I have recently become aware of how important it is that both Callie and I enjoy her toys. I have to play with them for hours on end, too.

February 17 — Sunday

QTY/ITEM	CAT	PRICE	TOTAL
10 Enfamil	sustenance	29.90	
2 4-pack ready-to-serve Enfamil	easier sustenance	13.98	
		$43.88	$8,736.49

February 18 — Monday

QTY/ITEM	CAT	PRICE	TOTAL
1 Jammy blanket	warmth that fits	4.98	
1 3-pack socks	increased footage	2.59	
1 Outfit	size 2!	4.97	
		$12.54	$8,749.03

February 19 — Tuesday

When you wake up due to a strange gurgling sound next to you and then you feel a nasty warm sensation and then you turn on the light and there is baby puke everywhere and a surprised and upset baby is staring at you with further substance spewing from her mouth, you can be pretty sure your baby has a stomach virus.

QTY/ITEM	CAT	PRICE	TOTAL
1 Doctor co-pay	vomit patrol	$15.00	$8,764.03

February 20 — Wednesday

When you come back from Weight Watchers and can't wait to tell your mom who is looking after your baby that you finally broke through your plateau thanks to lots of egg whites and no pancakes and you lost 3.8 pounds and you're only 2 pounds away from where you were when you first weighed in after getting pregnant but you can't tell anyone because the baby is crying in her crib and your mom's head is down the toilet, you can be pretty sure your mom caught the stomach virus from the baby.

February 21 — Thursday

When you leap from a sound sleep running full tilt with your hand clapped over your face and still you can't get to the toilet in time, you can be pretty sure you have the same stomach virus as your mom and your baby.

And when your significant other, who thus far has steadfastly refused to buckle, takes a brisk walk to the library only to puke on the library lawn, it's pretty clear he's got it, too.

Once again we are facing more than simple illness. We're fighting an army of evil little molecular germs that slam like Sonny Liston and fly at super-baby velocity.

On the other hand, Callie has introduced such a comprehensive and cost-free dietary aid into the environment that I feel ill at ease charging her for this week's Weight Watcher fee. While I do not feel a stomach virus makes for a healthy long-term weight-loss program, it certainly is effective in the short run when one is looking to nix that extra pound or two for a weekend at the beach, a wedding, or maybe your kid's first birthday.

Thank you, baby.

QTY/ITEM	CAT	PRICE	TOTAL
2 Cans lacto-free formula	digestive aid	$5.98	$8,770.01

February 23 — Saturday

Please Come to My Party

I'll be one.

～

WHO: Callie

WHEN: Thursday, March 14, 9 A.M. to 11 A.M.

WHERE: Mountainside Café

WHAT: My First Birthday Breakfast Bash

～

Come have the breakfast of your choice
Mom's paying and she says she won't bill me.
So, bon appyteet.
See ya there!

QTY/ITEM	CAT	PRICE	TOTAL
30 Color Xeroxes	birthday invitations	32.70	
2 Neon Slinkies	game prizes	5.98	
24 Party hats	festive heads	5.47	
1 2-lb bag piñata filler	party favor packs	8.99	
24 Noisemakers	festive sound	5.47	
1 Happy Birthday sign	festive decor	1.49	
4 Baby toys	party favors for the very young	11.48	
25 Pink balloons	festive air	1.49	
1 "1" Birthday candle	festive fire	1.19	
		$74.26	$8,844.27

February 25 — Monday

My next-door neighbor is pregnant. She's due in September. Callie will no longer be the baby in town.

You can't stay young forever.

February 26 — Tuesday

The digestive battle continues . . .

QTY/ITEM	CAT	PRICE	TOTAL
4 Cans lacto-free formula	stem the tide	$11.96	$8,856.23

February 27 — Wednesday

It was a very good day for Callie. My tax return is complete and Callie has decreased her debt by 23 percent thanks to a child credit, an additional exemption, and a change in my personal status to "head of household."

I know precisely how Callie's credits break out due to the fact that my tax attorney has caught wind of Callie's debt and is clearly distressed by the situation. She spent an additional twenty minutes this afternoon determining exactly how much of Callie's debt should be relieved in the name of the Internal Revenue Service.

Here are the numbers given to me (with a reprimanding look—did I imagine that?) by Martha Miller, tax attorney and defender of babies in financial crisis.

QTY/ITEM	CAT	PRICE	TOTAL
1 Child credit	TAX CREDIT	+ 600	
1 Exemption	TAX CREDIT	+ 797	
1 "Head of Household"	TAX CREDIT	+ 353	
1 State of CT	TAX CREDIT	+ 104	
1 State of NY	TAX CREDIT	+ 194	
		+ $2,048	($4,170.49)

Perhaps it's fatigue-induced paranoia but I'm beginning to sense that the people around me are developing an "us-against-them" attitude in regard to the tally. They have aligned themselves with Callie and call themselves "Us."

I am "Them."

February 28 — Thursday

QTY/ITEM	CAT	PRICE	TOTAL
1 Weight Watchers weekly fee	stomach-flu alternative	$10.55	$8,866.78

Puke for twenty-four hours. Eat soup for three days. Gain .4 pounds. Huh?

March 1 — Friday

Callie will be a one-year-old in two weeks. I want to feel like we're breaking over the crest of a great hill, that the sun is splitting open the sky, that together we are gracefully and effortlessly leaping across the threshold of a new world where children sleep through the night, cysts magically dissolve, and many teeth chew solid food.

But this is not the case. The child's sleep patterns are, at least, no better and possibly worse. She still has a small lump under her original scar and, in fact, I have postponed her return checkup from March 8 to the 23 so that we can travel home to Michigan to visit Grampa and clan (and get his medical opinion on the situation). And with regard to chewing, Callie continues to be the proud owner of two teeth—no more. This fact significantly limits the rate at which we can switch emphasis from bottle to bowl.

None of this is critical. We don't need resolution by her birthday. I just want it. I would like to feel a great cleansing breath wiping away the challenges of old and preparing for the battles ahead. I would enjoy the neat sense of order that that would create.

But Callie does not care. She prefers the organic approach—messy and process-oriented.

I must say, overall, this whole baby business has been very hard on my OCD. As if fifteen months without a full night's sleep isn't exhausting enough, you can't imagine how tiring it is to continually present yourself with the illusion that you are in control when, in fact, there is a very short czar running your home.

QTY/ITEM	CAT	PRICE	TOTAL
1 Aetna US Healthcare co-pay	czar insurance	15.29	
1 Vision @ $4.54	czar insurance	4.54	
		$19.83	$8,886.61

March 2 — Saturday

Gramma's birthday was yesterday. Unlike her granddaughter, she was somewhat older than one and in a bit of a funk thanks to that fact.

"I just wish you'd asked me yesterday how old I was so I could say sixty-five one more time."

Slam. Guilt. Well, how was I supposed to know that?

"Is sixty-six wildly different?" I asked.

"No. But when I get to seventy — if I get to seventy — you're going to have a basket case on your hands."

Slam. I'm trapped. There's no way out of this town.

"Don't tell me about basket cases," I snapped, "I'm staring down the barrel of forty."

"Ha!" Mom said.

"I'm sorry I didn't ask you how old you are. Are you still funked out?"

"No. I'm fine," she said without an ounce of sincerity.

Sometimes I get an itchy feeling under my fingernails. It's always a good indication that whatever I'm reacting to has no reasonable solution. One cannot scratch beneath a fingernail and one cannot direct Mom away from doom. She runs for it like a baby for candy. And she will wrestle with it until she is good and ready to be done. I know nothing I do or say will change her feelings and yet, every time, I do, I say. I try to change her feelings.

Without trying, Callie did the job. She got a smile and a nod for presenting a birthday basket of luxury food from Dean & Deluca.

QTY/ITEM	CAT	PRICE	TOTAL
1 Basket luxury food	gift	$47.39	$8,934.00

She got a coo and a laugh for getting all dolled up and joining us for a fancy restaurant birthday dinner where she fawned over her Gramma with hugs and giggles so that strangers smiled and nodded at her Gramma.

Most significantly, however, she got an utter meltdown for having apparently settled on a name for Gramma.

For reasons familial and personal, Mom really did not want to be called "Gramma Howie." And the name my brothers and I used for her mother, "Non," is so attached to Non that I, for one, could not make the leap to calling anyone else "Non." We have tested a long list of names over this last year—Grammy, Granny, Mammy, Grammalou—but nothing has rung true.

Mom kept saying, "Callie will decide."

I didn't realize the import of this until I watched Mom's face as we all realized that something Callie has been saying for several weeks now appears to be directly attached to her Gramma.

I have never seen my mother so purely pleased and tickled. Callie has decided to call her "Bob."

March 3 — Sunday

We get on an airplane in five days and Callie still has diarrhea. I am not pleased.

The doc on call promises that, although a baby's system gets far more out of whack than an adult's when it comes to things like the stomach flu, it should be cleared up by takeoff. Whatever. The whole thing has me wracked with anxiety.

Dr. Brown called from the middle of his vacation to suggest Isomil DF, a formula specifically designed for this kind of situation (gastric distress, not plane travel). He is particularly concerned that Callie be fully repaired by the fourteenth as he is planning to attend the Birthday Breakfast Fête and has rescheduled patients accordingly.

QTY/ITEM	CAT	PRICE	TOTAL
4 Cans Isomil DF	plan B	$24.36	$8,958.36

March 6 — Wednesday

QTY/ITEM	CAT	PRICE	TOTAL
1 Weight Watchers weekly fee	thrills/chills	$10.55	$8,968.91

Down 1 pound. In order to reach my Callie birthday goal, I must lose 1.2 pounds by next week.

The suspense is almost more than I can bear.

March 7 — Thursday

Remember that treadmill that George Jetson used to run on during the opening of *The Jetsons*? Remember when Astro the dog would jump on the treadmill and get it going so fast that George would end up getting sucked into the machine, whipped around and around, unable to stop it from spinning and unable to run as fast as it was going?

That's me, unable to run as fast as I'm going. It's perfectly clear to me now why hard-core working women who have the option of not working often throw in the career towel moments after returning from maternity leave. The everyday balance is not only precarious — it's heavy as hell. Add to that a trip to visit Grampa for which it takes three days to pack and four planes to make, a birthday party for a one-year-old that keeps evolving and of course, diarrhea that won't quit. Oh, and did I mention? Callie and I both happened upon a new cold virus yesterday.

When is spring?

Just keep running.

QTY/ITEM	CAT	PRICE	TOTAL
1 Porcelain piggy bank	grand prize — birthday party game	14.75	
1 Set baby beads	surprise element for plane ride	10.00	
4 Jars food	travel supplies	1.84	
3 Jars various chickens	protein attempts	2.77	

continued on next page

continued from previous page

2	Lacto-free formula, ready-to-use	convenience digestion	9.78
2	Lacto-free formula, condensed	economic digestion	6.38
1	Box Cheerios	the law	2.99
3	Boxes cookies	plane behavior bribes	4.77
1	Box rice cereal	another law	1.50
1	Jumbo pack Pampers	necessities	19.99
			————
			$74.77 $9,043.68

March 11 — Monday

QTY/ITEM	CAT	PRICE	TOTAL
1 Airport banana	snack	1.00	
1 Bottle fluoride	travel damage*	8.79	
1 Wipes	there's always something . . .	1.69	
		————	
		$11.48	$9,055.16

*I seem to have returned without the necessary fluoride.

It's not healthy to travel alone with a child. It accelerates deterioration of the physical, emotional, mental, and spiritual selves and there is absolutely nothing you can buy to make it better — except perhaps a nanny but then you're not traveling alone, are you? Alone, you are in for utter and unbillable de-

struction. Utter and unbillable are a bad combo—they so easily lead to bitterness and spite.

We have returned from a very successful visit to Michigan,
where Callie chattered away with Grampa, played stack-'em-
up-knock-'em-down-and-sort-'em-over-and-over with Wendy
(who has offered up the possible name of "WeeWee," to which
I say the jury is out), heard Aunt Sarah sing in her choir, had
breakfast with Cindy and Tammy, went for a drive with Diane,
barked at Bumper the dog, rode a carousel, made hand-print
plates, ate sushi, went shopping for a birthday outfit, posed for
579 pictures and never, ever once let go of her mother.

I would not make a good single mom. I require unionized
breaks.

Callie is a genuine joy. She's smart and beautiful—really,
that's not just me talking. She's funny and sweet and alert and
inquisitive. She even resolved her gastric disruption before we
got on the plane. There is nothing more she could do to be
more fabulous and still, I require breaks.

I can feel the bounce in my joints begin to give way after six
hours. I can hear the buzz of my brain cells expiring after
twelve. And then I go somewhere else, into a soft, numb kind
of bubble where I couldn't tell you what I said ten seconds after saying it. I remove myself, keeping only my physical person
in place so as to support the baby and keep her safe. The rest
of me goes to Barbados or Brooklyn or anywhere that isn't here.

I consider this shabby behavior on my part. I want to be
able to do this all day, every day, with a full and open heart.
But I am not that person—that selfless matron-saint. I crave
too much the company of my own thoughts.

I have a fair amount of guilt around this issue. Of course,
the child has already keyed into that fact and therefore under-

stands that her little shit-fits when I arrive at Gramma's to take her home can unravel me like a cheap sweater. She's pitched her fits several times now, wrapped her arms around her Bob and refused to even look at me unless she's screaming like a maniac.

This is where I'm supposed to realize that I have been negligent and selfish, unable to handle my own child for a twenty-four-hour period. I oblige. I also squelch little sparks of resentment toward my mother for being better at this than I am. She can stay with it all day long and give the appearance of actual enjoyment even after the 324th reading of *Witzy Plays Hide & Seek*.

She's deceiving, my mother, with her "Whatever you want, honey," and "Oh, I could never do that!" and "Ugh! I don't know how you handle everything you do, honey. I'd be exhausted."

Bull-honkey. The woman is made of steel. Her endurance is not human.

If the child would only nap. I hear other mothers talking about these one-hour, two-hour, more-hour breaks they get in the middle of their days and I think—well, then . . . then, I could do it. But Callie does not nap. Occasionally, she will rest her eyes for twenty minutes but this is not sleep. It's just the pulling down of her third reptilian lid through which she can obviously see because the second I attempt to focus on something other than her, she wakes up.

So, what are my choices? I can either mercilessly beat myself up or accept the fact that I am not a good full-time stay-at-homer and just be damn sure I never leave Lonnie and that my mother lives forever.

I remember, several years ago, bumping into an old boyfriend I hadn't seen in a very long time. We immediately went into that typical street-corner catch-up conversation. He asked me what I was doing, where I was living, and then he asked if I was single. I had just met Lonnie so I told the old boyfriend, "no." I said I'd met someone and I suspected we were in it for the long haul.

The old boyfriend raised his eyebrows and asked with anticipation, "Really? Who'd you get?"

I loved that question. I still do. It so completely acknowledges the random predetermined chaos that is at the center of every decision we consider "free will." Who'd you get? Pick a card, any card.

I'm who Callie got.

Callie's who I got.

I'm also who Lonnie got and vice versa. Dad's who Mom got even though eventually Wendy's who Dad got. Much as I got Lonnie after Lonnie got Julie but then Julie got Fred and so on. Mom got—well, I guess Mom got screwed since after Wendy got Dad, Mom got nobody. But then I got Callie and so did Mom. And she'd already gotten me and by association Lonnie much as I got Wendy and then we both got Sarah. And in return, they got Lonnie and everyone got Callie and so on and so on and so on. Amen. Amen. Amen.

There ain't no such thing as free will and we are all beholden.

March 12 — Tuesday

When Dad came to the airport last Friday to pick up Callie and me, we saw each other from a distance at first. I could see a tickled smile break across his face as he took in the size and depth of his granddaughter. But by the time he actually got to us, the nature of his smile had changed to something more considered.

"There's not much baby left," he said. "She looks like a little girl."

I am being flooded with flashback images all labeled, "A year ago right now . . ."

I can't stop figuring out what was happening right now one year ago today. For example, right now, I was already once-returned home from the hospital and was forcing my bloated self upright in order to walk around the block.

In four hours, my water will break.

Later —

Just as my broken water turned one, I weighed in at Weight Watchers to learn that I did not attain my goal. In fact, rather than losing anything this week, I went up .4 pounds.

I am working to take in the global view. I remind myself that over the course of a year, I lost a total of 38 pounds and came within 2 pounds of my goal. Over the course of the most challenging year of my life to date, I have come within reach of exactly what I want, have let go of what I don't, and accepted that those things that have not come to pass will do so on their own timetable — or not.

To which I practice saying, "Oh well."

QTY/ITEM	CAT	PRICE	TOTAL
1 Weight watchers weekly fee	the final charge	$10.55	$9,065.71

March 14 — Thursday

Let me tell you, turning one is not just about the cake.

There's also the checkup. (Thanks so much for yet another shot, Dr. Brown. One of these days, when I'm taller and have achieved upright balance, we're going to have it out about this needle business. In my opinion, your obsession is unhealthy.)

QTY/ITEM	CAT	PRICE	TOTAL
1 Doctor Visit	co-pay	$15.00	$9,080.71

And there is the day-to-day . . . a baby may be one but you still gotta eat.

QTY/ITEM	CAT	PRICE	TOTAL
6 Cans Enfamil	daily bread	$19.14	$9,099.85

There are the party games.

And there's your Dad, who needs special attention because sometimes he gets lost in the shuffle of so many women. He's standing just outside the circle looking in so you have to throw him a wave and a real slow blink so he knows you appreciate the fact that he's never charged you for a thing and never will. He'll always think you've more than paid your

Welcome to Callie's

First Birthday Breakfast Bash!

(Answer questions below. Return quiz to
Callie's assistant [Betsy] by 10:30 A.M.)

QUESTION #1:

One year ago today, Callies weighed 6 lbs. 14 ozs.
How much do you think she weighs today?

_____ lbs. _____ ozs.

QUESTION #2:

One year ago today, Callie was 21 inches long.
How long do you think she is today?

_____ inches

QUESTION #3:

One year ago today, Callie's debt was $2,747.60.
How much do you think she owes today?

$ _____

ANSWERS: #1: 19 lbs. 6½ ozs. (25th percentile) #2: 30¼ inches
long (80th percentile) #3: $9,099.85

way even when you're flat broke, fresh out of piggy banks, and begging for Zwieback.

And then there are the bittersweet wanderings of your mother's mind as she reviews again and again all you have been and done in the last twelve months. She will sit at your party two steps removed from the action. In fact, even if you happen to fall asleep before your cake comes out, you will still, in many ways, be more present than your mother.

She is wondering why the journal she kept of your first year is so unbalanced. She's considering the fact that it took twice as long to tell the first half of your story as it did to tell the second half. She realizes as she stares at the flame atop the "1" candle on your cake and you sleep soundly in your Gramma's arms that by your sixth month, she wasn't looking as carefully.

Mom suspects there is a grace in crisis — good crises as well as bad. It sharpens the focus and makes grown-ups live as they should, awash in detail and the anguished beauty of the moment to moment.

But it appears that after a while, no matter what befalls them, no matter what made them slow down to the rhythm of their own hearts, they eventually rise up and get running at the speed of life, which doesn't have time for a lot of detail. According to Mom, it's like trying to grab the specifics off a tunnel wall from a speeding subway car. She says looking at the detail makes a person's head hurt and her eyes go into a funky jitter dance.

Personally, I enjoy a funky jitter dance.

So does Bob. She's the finest funky jitter dancer I know.

That's one of the details I think Mom missed. Otherwise, she wouldn't worry so much about Bob, about whether she's making friends, exercising enough, doing the things that Mom thinks will make Bob happy. She's afraid Bob's lonely and depressed.

I don't think Mom's seen Bob do the jitter dance. I think she sees some dance Bob used to do before she learned her funky new moves.

I've never seen the old dance. I am the queen of the here and now. If you're looking to start over, I'm a safe bet. I cannot tell you how things have been, I can only tell you the way they are.

And Bob is better than anyone else in the world at handing me beads and counting up colors and finding empty food containers. She is an expert Jell-O maker and when we're alone, she dances. She does the funky jitterdance and it makes me laugh until I fall over and cry.

She also whispers secrets to me that I am not at liberty to reveal but I can assure you that Bob is not sad. Bob is just fine.

And Mom will be just fine, too—eventually.

Soon I will start to talk and then I won't be so all-knowing, but for the moment, when I take a look around me, I see the greater truths behind everything. And Mom is starting to come around.

She made a wish when my candle got blown out—to live forever the two of us, to let the party go on and on.

Now she's smiling at me, not that half-wit smile that's supposed to get me to laugh but a real person-to-person smile because she's finally connecting the dots.

Today is our birthday. This is her party as much as mine, and I'm her ticket to never having to leave. I'm her all-night-hand-stamp pass. Thanks to me, she'll be staying past dawn and on into forever.

I'd like a second opinion on this debt.

For my birthday, I got: orange tennis shoes, brown boots, blue dress shoes and one pair of slippers, a pink jumper, a blue dress with green frogs, a pink parka, a blue sweater, three stuffed dogs, a no-mess finger paint board, a tan bear, a pair of pink loafers, a brown plush bear, a black bear, a book about a cat, a wooden peg sorting cube, a fuzzy blue elephant, a bouquet of yellow flowers, a green two-in-one xylophone crocodile, a wooden pound-n-roll toy, blue pants, a white sweater, one hot-pink flowered ensemble, a Treasure of Fairy Tales, *a complete collection of Pooh stuffed animals, six hardcover books, two with paper pages, four green bathtub frogs, and a fine red Fisher Price car.*

Mom got: her wish.

> *Credits:* $4,170.49
> *Disbursements:* $9,099.85

Addendum

~

Total Cost of
Baby's First Year

Cost of billed expenses for Baby's First Year: $9,099.85*

see pages 1–319 for details

Value of Gifts, Complimentary and Insured Items

	GIFTS	COMPS	INSURED	TOTAL
Clothes	2,945.31	142.04		
Shoes	392.41	32.00		
Toys	1,314.39	55.99		
Publications	907.99			
Furniture	614.99			
Kitchenware	487.90			
Room decor	454.99			
Bedding and dry goods	321.91			
Toiletries	347.27			
Equipment	390.87			
Transportation	34.90			
Other stuff	81.97	490.00*		
Gift certificates	100.00			
Medical			7,884.81	
Subtotal	$8,394.90	$720.03	$7,884.81	$16,999.74

Parties in the child's honor.

Grand Total of all billed and non-billed expenses:
$26,099.59

A CONVERSATION
WITH BETSY HOWIE

~

*About herself, Callie, writing, acting,
shopping binges, patience, and grace.*

Where did you grow up?
I grew up in Grand Rapids, Michigan. We also had a summerhouse
on the lake in northern Michigan. But no matter where I was, I was
not where I felt I belonged, which was New York or Hollywood. I
would have taken either over Grand Rapids.

Why?
I wanted to be an actress. I started getting *Variety* when I was eleven.
I mostly wanted it so I could cut out the audition notices that listed
parts that were "perfect" for me. I'd post them on the fridge so my
parents would know precisely what they were keeping me from by
living in Grand Rapids.

So, did you ever make it to Hollywood?
No, but I made it to New York. I went to New York University and

majored in drama. Then, while I was at NYU, I started writing plays, because that's the form I was buried in.

After I graduated, I continued writing lots and lots of plays. I also had 157 jobs that had nothing do with writing or acting—selling hot-dogs, waitressing, bartending, video production, event management, publicity, speech writing. I once wrote a speech for Ronald and Nancy Reagan. I drove a golf cart for Walter Cronkite. I was a pub-licist for the Dalai Lama. I was Stella Adler's personal assistant. Mixed in were lots and lots of unpaid or meagerly paid Off-Off-Broadway performances, occasional extra work on one soap opera or another, and loads of strange performances of my own solo stuff in dark black rooms in lower Manhattan. Eventually, the pay improved. I got into commercials. I wrote the book for the musical *Cowgirls* that ran off-Broadway, and I acted in that as well.

I'm actually working on a performance version of *Callie's Tally* right now. I've cut a three-hundred-some-page book down to about eighty pages while trying not to lose its soul, in order to transform it into a doable one-woman performance piece.

I've always thought that the book is at its best, people's responses are the best, when I read it out loud. That's when people really get it. They get the humor behind it, and they get the love. Of course, a lot of people get this on their own. But I know that whenever I read it out loud, no one walks away thinking that this is serious, that this is some sort of accounting book.

What originally inspired you to write Callie's Tally?

I was five months' pregnant and walking out of the store after my first shopping spree for the baby. I had spent six-hundred–some dol-lars! And I had this flash—this being inside me now has "stuff." It was such a weird thought. It made her so real. Then I started won-dering why I was paying for this stuff if it was all hers. That made me laugh enough to want to write down the words I was thinking. So I did, and I read it out loud to some of my friends at work—women of all different ages, women with children and without—and they were all laughing. So I just kept going.

Also, one of my main terrors about having a child was the prospect of losing my creative life. So I thought, maybe this is the *one* kind of writing that I might be able to manage during the first year of the baby's life—little snippets here and there about the baby, about being a parent. I certainly knew that I couldn't write a novel during that time. I wouldn't have that kind of focus.

What is the difference between writing a novel and writing something like Callie's Tally?

For one thing, writing a novel means you have to come up with a story line. That's the hardest thing for me—coming up with a plot. You also have to come up with characters and motivations, figure out what makes them tick, and make the whole thing interesting but not too obvious and not too complex. In my first year with Callie, I didn't have enough RAM to do that. I didn't have enough brain cells or focus.

On the other hand, with writing *Callie's Tally*, the biggest challenge was to be as honest as possible, so the real emotional life came through. I was so raw during that first year that getting to the truth was pretty easy.

Writing that book was also therapy for me. It helped me to keep my sanity after Callie was born. It forced me to step back and find humor in the moments of those really horrible days, when my breasts were about to explode and I was wetting my pants and I was exhausted all the time. I found that first year so difficult. I know some people think that that first year is the best year. But it was an endurance test for me. I kept telling myself to just hang in there and

make it to the end, to the time when she would be a little more inde-
pendent, and I could get my arms back.

Was that first year harder than you thought it would be?
Maybe it was a kind of self-protection. But before I had the baby, I
never thought to myself, "What would an actual day of parenting be
like?" I looked at it in very broad sweeps. I never really got down to
the nitty-gritty until I was in the middle of it. And it was unbelievable! I didn't have a second to myself.

I don't know what I would have done if my mother hadn't moved
across the country to help me with the baby. My mother gave me
time every day to sort of sit and stare. I remember when I was alone
in my house for the first time since I'd had the baby. I thought, "*Oh,
my god*, it's been a long time!"

You said that you were very raw while you were writing the first draft of
Callie's Tally. *While you were working on later drafts, were you ever
tempted to edit out or censor out some of that rawness?*
I was really more worried about whether or not the book would make
people laugh! The thing that *did* make me sometimes cringe was, what
did I say about someone else? Because I had put family members in
the book. So that's the tweaking I did—what I said about other people.

How did Callie's dad feel about the book?
He was very supportive. He's a playwright himself. He was really
cool about it all, considering that he was pushed around a bit in the
book!

What was your writing routine like after the baby was born?
Up until she was born, I wrote whenever I wanted to write. It got
really hard right after she was born. I depended on my mother to

hold her for a few minutes so I could jot down some notes here and there. I'd write them up whenever I could steal a moment.

It was also emotionally tough to write during that time. I had gone through this unbelievable physical ordeal. And then I had this incredibly needy, trusting, dependent person. I felt so vulnerable, so weepy. I had difficulty maintaining that tough-nosed tone that I'd started with the book before she was born. I knew I had to be honest with how I was feeling, but not go so far into "sappy" that it became a different kind of book.

Eventually, I ended up thinking of that part of the book—Callie's first months—as one of the best parts of the book. Because it does have that double-edged quality. I was slowly recovering my humor.

I went back to work part-time in New York City when Callie was about three and a half months old. That commuting time saved my personal writing routine. I wrote a lot of *Callie's Tally* while I was on the train.

What is your job? How does it fit into your weekly routine?

Tuesdays and Thursdays, I work at Scholastic Inc. in New York City. I do a number of things—running student contests through the Book Clubs and promotional writing. I'm also a freelance writer for them. I write books for various series: Scooby-Doo, Pokémon, Power-puff Girls, Dexter's Laboratory, Lizzie McGuire, Wild Thornberrys. I write them under a pseudonym: Howie Dewin.

Mondays, Wednesdays, and Fridays, I have Callie with me except for about two and a half hours when she goes over to Min's. That's the latest official name for Grandma. The nickname Bob, which was in the book, didn't last. My mother thinks Callie calls her Min because she's always saying, "Just a minute!" to Callie.

During those two and a half hours, I do work for Scholastic, I do my own writing, I pay bills, I squeeze in what I can. Then, in the afternoons, Callie and I try to find something to do. Fridays, she has a play group with her pals.

Do you still keep a tally of Callie's expenses?
No! I was so glad not to have to sort through receipts after her first birthday.

How do you think Callie will react when she reads your book someday?
She's got a real-live sense of humor. This isn't just her mom talking. She's really funny. I have no doubt she'll "get" the book. I'm sure that at some points she'll use it against me—but in the end, when she's grown up, she'll realize that it's just a love letter to her. It's the ultimate baby book.

I've asked my mother so many times: "What was I like when I was this age or that age? What did my brothers and I do?" I still ask her. But she doesn't remember. Most mothers don't. They're so overwhelmed that they can't hold on to all those details.

I, on the other hand, was forced to, at least for that first year. So Callie has a record of how she became *her.*

So even if this book had never gotten published or sold a single copy, she would still have that. It's a gift to her.

Callie's Tally *involves three generations of mothers and daughters. Do you think of it as a "mother-daughter" book? Would it have been a different book if you'd had a boy instead of a girl?*
The book definitely took on a mother-daughter-relationship angle, since Callie was a girl baby and because my mother moved across the country to be a full-time part of our lives. It was inevitable that it would end up addressing the ways in which mothers and daughters

owe each other, on all kinds of levels. But I don't think that takes away from the universality of "parent-child." Most of the mountains you climb during that first year are gender-free.

Do you feel, deep down, that our children "owe" us in some way?
What I feel deep down, is that we all owe each other. I mean that in the epic sense—not in the familial. But it all starts with the family, doesn't it?

One of my favorite passages in *Callie's Tally* is about that: "I'm who Callie got. Callie's who I got. I'm also who Lonnie got and vice versa. Dad's who Mom got even though eventually Wendy's who Dad got. Much as I got Lonnie after Lonnie got Julie but then Julie got Fred and so on. Mom got—well, I guess Mom got screwed since after Wendy got Dad, Mom got nobody. But then I got Callie and so did Mom. And she'd already gotten me and by association Lonnie much as I got Wendy and then we both got Sarah. And in return, they got Lonnie and everyone got Callie and so on and so on and so on. Amen. Amen. Amen. There is no such thing as free will and we are all beholden."

It's a thought that comforts me.

When you were growing up, did you have a sense of how much or how little money your parents were spending on you? What were their attitudes about money?
I would say that my parents were very fiscally conscious. But our family didn't discuss money. It wasn't polite.

I remember early on, my mother became the "Bank of Mom." My brothers and I had a weekly allowance. She kept this little book with deposits and withdrawals. One brother was always in the red. The other brother always had tons and tons of money. I was always in the middle.

Are you still like that now? Not poor, not rich, but somewhere in the middle?

I guess that's where I am now. Though I'm aware that on a global scale, I'm very, very fortunate. But in my estimation, I'm hardly rolling in it. I'm just "okay."

I do have to battle the money demon. I can get very anxiety-ridden over money. You want to think money's not important, but it is. You want to think it's not what makes or breaks. But how many relationships can you think of where ultimately, the breaking point is money? It's awful, but it's the reality.

When I was in my twenties, I was the only one of my artistic-acting-Lower-East-Side-of-New York set that had a savings account. I have a college fund now for Callie, which I add to whenever I can. When it comes to money, I'm very compulsive, anal-retentive, whatever you want to call it. It's all a mechanism to try to cope with anxiety.

In your book, you talk about your need to control everything. But having a child is so much about being out of control. What has having Callie taught you about that?

Callie has reached that point where I am forced to acknowledge that there are at least two different ways of measuring time: Real Time (i.e., the way I measure it), and Callie Time (i.e., way slower). For example: According to my watch, it should take about seventeen and a half seconds to exit the house, walk the forty-two steps to the barn, step into the barn, walk the eleven steps to the car, get into the car, and fasten the seat belt.

But Callie sees it more as an afternoon outing. There are hats to try on before exiting the house; things to pick at while standing at the threshold of the door; many natural objects and creatures to touch on the way down the walk; games to play on the two steps into the barn;

bicycles and other various modes of transportation to test while in the garage; and seven different ways to climb into the car seat.

Some days, I'm just fine about it. But often, it takes everything in me not to scoop her up and say, "WE DON'T HAVE TIME!" While sometimes that's true, just as often it's my own rushed sense of life and my maniacal need to control it clouding my vision. In those moments, I have to take a deep breath and not rush her right past 13,000 opportunities to form her opinion of the world.

Callie is the biggest lesson I've had in not being able to control everything. I'll be learning that lesson all my life. The thing is to accept this lesson with grace.

Have you reached grace yet?
No. But I wish for it all time. Grace and tranquillity.

Are you spending more money on her now then you did when she was younger?
Less. I definitely had some shopping binges back then. I went out and bought her ridiculous amounts of clothes. There was a point when I was so disgusted with myself, I couldn't even write about it.

Why did you do so much shopping?
It was the first time in my life that I really got that shopping *thing*. I actually felt better after I bought stuff. Plus, shopping was one activity I could do with Callie. Also, girl's clothes are so cute.

There was also an insecurity factor. Back then, I felt that I had to buy a lot of stuff for her in order to be a good parent. Now, I don't feel like I need to buy seven million things for her to take care of her.

In the beginning, what costs shocked you the most?
I didn't get shocked by the one-time things, like car seats. It was

more the daily or weekly expenses like diapers and formula that really shot through the roof.

Has Callie gotten to the age when she asks for things at the store?
Yeah, and I give in. What replaced the clothes are endless, stupid little toys. We were at the pharmacy the other day, and I bought this flashlight for her where she presses a button and the light comes on while a bunny twirls around. Absolutely useless. I also bought her a hammer recently that makes a sound when you hit it. $2.99. All this accumulation of useless things goes against everything I've ever believed. It's so American. It's so gross. But it makes her smile.

Do you spend a lot of money on yourself?
I'm not a shopping person. I get headaches at the mall. Still, I do spend more than I used to. I'm stressed a lot. I'm juggling a lot. So sometimes, I'll go online and buy something that I wouldn't have bought in the old days. It makes me feel better.

Before you wrote Callie's Tally, you asked yourself five questions about the prospect of having a baby. The first question was, "Can I physically handle it?" Now that you've had Callie, how would you answer that question?
The answer is yes. I mean, it's been hard, and it took me a long time to lose the weight. I'm just now back to my old weight. Also, I'm forty. I get tired with the baby but probably, so does a twenty-year-old . . . maybe just not quite *as* tired. And I look older than I did. Having a baby has definitely aged me. But I have physically been able to handle it, for the most part.

How about the second question: "Do I have the patience for the job?"
I have more patience than I thought I would have. I see young par-

ents on the train, yelling at their kids, freaking out on them. I totally get it. But I don't do that. There are times Callie is doing something that's incredibly annoying, but I just hold back. When I was younger, I couldn't have done that; I would have flipped out on her. That's not to say I'm patient all the time. I'm not patient by nature.

I also remember worrying that I wouldn't be able to endure the tedium of having a baby. There is so much tedium. I would watch friends with their two-year-olds, reading the same stories seventeen times, and I thought, "How can I do that?" But I don't mind doing that now, you know, reading the same stories seventeen times. When it's your own child, you realize that each moment, each experience, is only a split second. It all goes so fast.

How about: "Can I have my career and take care of my baby?"

Yes and no. I don't do commercials anymore. Not that there was any great artistic fulfillment in doing commercials, but that's gone. I tried to get back into it, but it wasn't worth the time I'd be away from Callie.

I miss being in the world of acting. But hopefully, this *Callie's Tally* workshop will happen, and I can have a taste of that again.

So the answer is, I *can* have my career, but I don't get it just when I want it in the way that I want it.

How about: "Will I be able to sidestep my own neuroses and negativity enough to raise an at least slightly healthy human being?"

You'll have to check back with me in twenty, thirty years. Right now, that is totally unanswerable.

The truth is, I'm even *more* neurotic and anxious since I had Callie. I worry more. I worry about the world, I worry about money, I worry about her safety, I worry about my safety.

Still, there are moments when I have this total calm that I never, ever had before. There's a deeper sense of everything—a better sense of what's important, what's not important. Sometimes at night, when I'm lying in bed with her, I feel like I'm exactly where I'm supposed to be, doing exactly what I'm supposed to be doing. You don't get that feeling often.

How about the last question: "Do I have enough money?"
Yes. So far, anyway.

How old is Callie now?
She'll be two this Friday. We're having a little birthday party at this café on Main Street in our little Connecticut town. It's a breakfast affair, with a bagel buffet.

There will be twenty to twenty-five people there, adults and kids. Last year, there was a quiz. She weighed this much at birth, what does she weigh now? She owed this much at birth, what does she owe now? This year's quiz is: "Talk Like Two: Can You Do It?" The guests will have to translate what Callie says. We'll see how that goes.

Don't tell her, but we got her a tricycle. It's one of those classic red Radio Flyers.

Callie inspired you to write Callie's Tally. *Has she inspired you creatively in other ways?*
She's given me a lot of ideas for children's books. For example, I want to write a children's book called *Mama's Pockets*. Everything you need is in Mama's pockets. Things go in, things come out, but there's never a question that what you need is in Mama's pocket—it's magic. I also have this idea to write a play using her vocabulary. I've been keeping lists of the words she knows, the new words she learns. Really, kids give you a whole new world of ideas.

But I'm working on something else right now. It's fiction for adults. I have about thirty pages. I don't know what it is yet. I have this character who is haunting me. I'm not sure who she is yet, though, or what she wants, or where she's going.

How do you balance your personal writing with other types of writing?
I think what's best is to have a little bit of work, freelance work, that's not your own personal work. That gives you some money as well as a structure for your day. Once you get that freelance work out of the way, you have the wide expanse of the day to do your personal writing.

Do you have that now?
I don't have the wide expanse of a *minute*.

When do you think you'll have the "wide expanse of a day" thing again?
Let's see, Callie is two. She'll be eighteen in sixteen more years. Check back with me then.

MORE FOOD FOR THOUGHT

~

12 Questions to Ask Yourself
(and Your Book Club Friends) About Callie's Tally

1. What parts of *Callie's Tally* resonated the most for you? Did you identify with Betsy Howie's parenting issues, money issues, both, or neither?

2. How did you feel about the "what my daughter owes me" subtitle of *Callie's Tally?* Did it make you laugh? Did it offend you? If the latter, why? Did you feel that Howie was literally saying that Callie owed her money, or was she saying something else?

3. Do you ever find yourself keeping a tally on what you give to the people in your life—children, friends, family members, significant others, coworkers? Deep down, does giving them something—whether it's your money, your time, your affection, or something else—make you feel that "they owe me"?

4. In her interview, Howie repeats a line from *Callie's Tally* that "we are all beholden" to each other, whether in a familial sense or a broader sense. What does this line mean to you? Do you agree with it?

5. Do you ever find yourself feeling the need to buy things for your children or for other people in your life in order to *prove* something to them—e.g., that you love them, that you're capable of taking care of them, etc.? Do you feel that you need people to buy things for you in order for you to feel loved by them? Where do these feelings and attitudes come from?

6. How does *Callie's Tally* differ from other baby books or parenting books you've read?

7. How does *Callie's Tally* differ from other memoirs or autobiographies you've read?

8. In her interview, Betsy Howie said that she wrote about Callie's first months while she was very weepy, vulnerable, and emotionally raw. Did that emotional rawness come through in that part of the book? In what ways? Did you feel that that part of the book was more "honest"?

9. What challenges do you think Betsy Howie had in writing a memoir that mentioned friends and family members? If you were to write your own memoir, do you think you could be totally frank and candid in describing your friends and family members, even if it meant saying negative or unflattering things?

10. In her interview, Betsy Howie described *Callie's Tally* as a "love letter" to Callie. Did you see the book this way? If you have small children, can you imagine writing a

book like *Callie's Tally* for and about them? What sorts of things would you write about?

11. Imagine that your mother, father, or other close, older family member had written a book about you when you were little, and you were able to read it for the first time now. What would this book be like? What sorts of things would be in this book? How would you feel reading it?

12. Do you think *Callie's Tally* is a mother-daughter book? Would it be a different book if Howie had had a boy instead? Do you think mothers of boys would enjoy reading this book as well as mothers of girls? Do you think fathers would enjoy it as well?

ABOUT THE AUTHOR

Betsy Howie is a novelist, playwright, and actress. Previous productions and publications of her writing include the Off-Broadway musical *Cowgirls* as well as the novel *Snow*. She has also written more than two dozen children's books under the pen name Howie Dewin. She lives in Connecticut.